WHAT PEOPLE ARE SAYIN(

ENLIGHTENMENT AIN'T WHAT IT'S CRACKED UP TO BE

Enlightenment ain't what it's cracked up to be *is a bone-deep description of the decades-long spiritual journey of Robert K. C. Forman, one of America's most respected spiritual teachers. If ever a book was written from the heart, this is it. It is both a summation and an update of a work in progress.* Enlightenment Ain't What It's Cracked Up to Be *describes the dazzling heights of spiritual awareness, but it also lays bare the twists, turns, and surprises of spiritual maturation, warts and all. Beware: If you need your spiritual guide to be serious, elevated, reserved, and pious, go elsewhere. But if you want eye-ball to eye-ball honesty, integrity, and humor super-charged with compassion, love, vulnerability, and deep wisdom, this is your book.*
Larry Dossey, MD. Author: *Healing Words and The Power of Premonitions*

This book is more than a memoir of a profoundly revealing spiritual journey. It is a deep invitation to be your authentic self--to fully own, embody and express every aspect of yourself. The honesty, openness and transparency of Robert's spiritual journey instantly captivated me. I read the book in one long, joyous sitting. I literally could not put the book down. It is illuminating, entertaining and impactful. If your looking for guidance as to what is truly spiritual and enlightening, then read this book.

It is definitely chicken soup for the spiritual seeker's soul!
Jack Canfield, Co-creator of the New York Times #1 bestselling *Chicken Soup for the Soul series*

Bob Forman's Enlightenment Ain't What It's Cracked Up to Be *is especially recommended for its honesty, openness, insight, wisdom, and significance. Points he brings up—in a thoroughly enjoyable memoir-type format—are absolutely central to the furtherance of this dialogue. Pick it up, give it a read, and ponder deeply its points—you won't regret it!"*

I loved it.

Ken Wilber, Author of Integral SpiritualityKen Wilber, Author of *Integral Spirituality*

What Robert Forman has learned about and accomplished in spiritual growth is inspiring. But even more than a touching personal memoir, Forman opens our thinking to new ideas of what 'enlightenment' or spiritual growth could actually be in the modern world. This is a vitally important issue: we have more to do in saving our world and our selves than learn to sit around in a cave feeling good and looking holy like the ancients did. Enlightenment Ain't What It's Cracked Up to Be *is a great book.*

Dr. Charles T. Tart, Author *States of Consciousness, and The End of Materialism: How Evidence of the Paranormal is Bringing Science and Spirit Together.*

Robert K.C. Forman offers a touching, humorous, and honest account of ordinary and extraordinary spiritual events. Relevant to anyone interested in the scientific exploration of what still remains mysterious.

Angeles Arrien, Ph.D, Cultural Anthropologist, Author of *The Second Half of Life: Opening the Eight Gates of Wisdom*

Some spiritual memoirs are so authentic, honest and well-told that they stir the soul. Others offer trenchant observations and wise commentary about the modern spiritual scene. This is one of the rare books that do both. Compelling, intriguing and thought-provoking, it is a graceful exposition of one man's journey, but it illuminates the path that millions are embarked upon.

Philip Goldberg, Author of *American Veda: From Emerson to the Beatles, How Indian Spirituality Changed the West*

Enlightenment Ain't What It's Cracked Up To Be *is a powerful breath of spiritual fresh air! It is one of the most refreshingly authentic accounts of the spiritual life I've ever read. In its clarity, honesty and depth, this book is the real deal. From the first page you are in conversation, encouraged to encounter and re-examine your own journey into how to integrate your spirituality with the rest of your life. Forman's extraordinary blend of personal courage, psychological awareness, formal cross-cultural philosophical training and direct spiritual experience is as unusual in the spiritual marketplace as it is helpful.*
Melissa Gayle West, M.S., LMHC, Author: of: *Exploring the Labyrinth: A Guide for Healing and Spiritual Growth*

Robert K.C. Forman does a beautiful job of linking spiritual autobiography with discussion of what it means to be on a spiritual path and engaged in personal development. Self-revealing and extremely well-written, it takes on the hard issues of the spiritual path and treats them with wisdom. This is definitely a book that I'd buy, for it makes the case that our conventional spiritual understanding is too simple for the complex lives we now lead. Enlightenment Ain't What It's Cracked Up to Be *stands head and shoulders above most other spiritual writings.*
Paul Ray, Ph.D. Author, *The Cultural Creatives*

Enlightenment Ain't What It's Cracked Up To Be

A Journey of Discovery, Snow and Jazz in the Soul

Enlightenment Ain't What It's Cracked Up To Be

A Journey of Discovery, Snow and Jazz in the Soul

Robert K. C. Forman, Ph.D.

Winchester, UK
Washington, USA

First published by O-Books, 2011
O-Books is an imprint of John Hunt Publishing Ltd., Laurel House, Station Approach,
Alresford, Hants, SO24 9JH, UK
office1@o-books.net
www.o-books.com

For distributor details and how to order please visit the 'Ordering' section on our website.

ISBN: 978 1 84694 674 5

A CIP catalogue record for this book is available from the British Library.

Design: Stuart Davies

Printed in the UK by CPI Antony Rowe
Printed in the USA by Offset Paperback Mfrs, Inc

CONTENTS

In the end what matters most is
How well did you live?
How deeply did you love?
How much did you give?
And how well did you learn to let go?

To Avram Michael Kraus Forman

son of

Robert Kraus-Conrad Forman

son of

Leonard Forman

son of

Morris Robert Forman

son of

Isaac Forman

son of…

May you be the first in your lineage to live jazz in the soul on the settled ground of spiritual spaciousness

Acknowledgements

It's hard to know who to thank for the life lessons represented in this book. Maharishi Mahesh Yogi stands out for the gift of silence he gave so many of us. So does Meister Eckhart, who from 700 years ago helped me connect the dots between the inner life and our outer *eigenschafts,* attachments. So does my twenty year rent-a-mom Ken Ruge and Ram Dass for being in the right place at the right time. I will be eternally grateful to my challenging mentor Wayne Proudfoot, whose tough love never allowed me to rest until the very end, and to the beloved Dr. Raffle, who nurtured my first curiosity as a farmer does a seed. I thank all my intrepid students at Vassar and Hunter College, who wondered with my wondering.

I am grateful to Doug Kruschke for teaching me how to find silence with another human being consistently. To Michael Schwartz and Mary Ellen Trahan, for being wise and thoughtful and sincere in a world that doesn't have nearly enough authenticity like theirs. I thank Michal Stryker for helping me discover a possibility I hadn't known existed. To my Swedish friends, especially Ted Harris, Inger Gustaffson Agneta Larson, and Marianne Blom, *tack för att du hjälper mig att gå djupt samtidigt som du gick djupt med mig.*

The book began in hours of conversation with Connie Zweig, who, I was surprised to discover, found it interesting enough to encourage me. I am deeply grateful for her open heartedness and curiosity. And to my dear friend Chris Schaefer, who was willing to listen to the other side of my journey so clearly and lovingly. Larry Dossey, Paul Ray and Charlie Tart and wife read earlier drafts and offered encouragement when it was most needed.

A special word of thanks to several dear, dear friends: Phil Goldberg, for being a lifelong friend, editor, teacher and Forge Institute colleague. To my friend Melissa West, feral and luscious Bodhisattva that she is, with whom I have shared, taught, learned and laughed with truth. To Tom Feldman, dear friend, Forge board chair and profoundly integrated soul, who in responding to draft after draft of this book has remained honest, insightful, truthful, tough and encouraging when I needed it; in everything he does, he calls me, and everyone he encounters, upwards.

My agent, Barbara Neighbors Deal, has become a welcome partner in navigating the blizzard that is publishing and marketing. Thanks to John Hunt, publisher extraordinaire, for amazingly helpful comments. And my thanks to Hans Jonassen for his clear sanity about the process of clarifying what readers will gain.

Finally how can I ever thank my lifelong partner, questioner, lover and best friend Yvonne Kraus Conrad Forman, or my wonderful, funny, hard working, challenging, gratifying children Rosha and Avram Forman?

For all these people, and for all who have taught me what it means to stand up straight, with your feet planted deep in the earth, and play jazz in the soul, a deep and heartfelt bow of gratitude.

Prologue

This is the tale of a man who got the pot of gold—of the spiritual persuasion—for which he had longed, and discovered that it wasn't what it had been cracked up to be. But who, over decades, realized that he had indeed been given a pot of gold, only it was of a kind and nature wholly different than anything he could have known to wish for.

It is also the ruminations of a lifetime of coming to understand what he had been given and the nature of the path to it that he, and perhaps all spiritual seekers today, are actually after.

And through it all, it is an effort to tell the truth. We live in an age of memoirs. Often when people tell of spiritual journeys like mine, or of others who undertake such journeys, they tend to idealize or demonize the tale, making it seem bigger or smaller than it was. Doing either squeezes out the sweaty ambiguity that soaks the fabric of every life. Confusion and pride and paradox and disappointment and unexpected possibility always, I suspect, come with this sort of journey. A spiritual life, even a so called enlightened spiritual life, is much less—and much more—than any self serving or bitter account could ever portray.

For spirituality is a field of grand illusions, peopled seemingly by angels or demons. Men and women undertake its rigors in part because of its promise, the utterly perfected life. It turns out that such a promise of perfect illumination is dishearteningly false. Yet we undertake such paths because there's also gold in them, we sense—something real, long term, and important. But once we step beyond the self talk and the hype, it's not clear just what that real gold might be: What is real human fulfillment? What is the good life? What gold, really, are we after in the complex lives we live? And how do we get *that*?

Such questions are far too important to be debated on the basis of highly inaccurate sound bites or mythologized hagiographies.

And so it is my goal here to tell the truth, the real truth, about the spiritual life: glories, warts, ecstasies, struggles and all. I want to share my research, my experience and my discoveries with you, as simply and as clearly as I am able.

Sometimes this means I will relay personal stories in ways that are anything but self-serving. Sometimes, frankly, they are embarrassing. Occasionally I will also tell of others in ways that may be less than complimentary. Those names I could change, I have. Some identities I cannot hide. If, in my efforts to tell the truth, I have hurt someone's feelings, I sincerely apologize.

On the other hand, telling the truth will also occasionally mean that I will describe certain of my and others' experiences and insights in ways that some may see as self-glorifying or exaggerated. Let me only say that, here too I have tried to write the truth as simply and as clearly as I am able. My goal throughout will be to tell my story and to share my conclusions about the spiritual path and goal as I have come to know them, and to speak of the promises, dangers and possibilities of a spiritual life as honestly as I am able.

In the spirit of such honesty, however, I am terribly aware that, from the title of this book through every page, I am challenging something that is, for many millions, a much beloved and central hope. Terms like enlightenment, heaven, Christ consciousness, nirvana and salvation, as I know first-hand, offer a *telos,* a spiritual aspiration. They say a perfect life is possible, that we can transcend our own egos, that we can live without pain and that our days can be filled with ease and love. Such hopes served to magnetize me, and many millions, towards self-transcendence. They hold out a powerful promise and life-compass.

There are such things as enlightenment, Christ Consciousness, nirvana and the like. These *are* worth working towards, *are* better to have than not. This is half of my life's conclusion. But they are not the panacea towards which I and so many have staked our lives. This is the other half. Enlightenment ain't what it has been cracked up to be.

Enlightenment is also far deeper, touching on the metaphysical, than we'd expect from the kind of positive thinking, be in the moment, personality-shifting teachings that dominates the spiritual marketplace today. Tools that are designed to change one's thought patterns and habits of character are useful; they can help us be more happy, stable or content. They work well for many. But they do not point to the kind of metaphysical shift that takes place *beneath* what we can know or how we know it which enlightenment does. The peculiar silence into which enlightenment shifts us is that *for which* there is self talk and personality changes, remembering and forgetting. Transformations at this level come by grace, not by self-adjustment. And it is time we stopped mistaking the content for the awareness that beholds it, the food for the tray.

Yet to say this, I know, is to challenge the existential orientation of many lives, some very deep shibboleths, and, to be realistic, perhaps the income of many spiritual teachers. I am fully aware of the gravity of the challenge I am hereby issuing. I do so humbly.

But the thought that you can be utterly ego-less, that you can remember to attend to your thought processes often enough to change them, that your guru is utterly egoless, that your everyday life is or will be both complete and entirely easy and that these are or should be our goals, has been a damaging fantasy, at best, and counter-productive at worst. I have written his book because it is high time that we turned around and looked squarely in the maw of our own daydreams. Here too the truth can set us free.

Part I.
Discovering It, Dismissing It

Chapter 1

Both / And It

I am writing from my meditation hermitage in the Catskill Mountains of upstate New York. I've never come in winter before. It's blazing cold. I'll be here longer than I've ever stayed. And I've never had to regulate the wood burning stove that dominates the downstairs. Even worse, I had the foolish idea that I should come here to write a book, but I'm scared that I will have nothing to say and that I will fail—miserably, embarrassingly, fail. So much for being the noble ascetic writer alone in his garret!

If I tell the real truth, as I hereby vow to do throughout this book, just now I'm anxious. I am thinking about a comfortable bed and a heating system that turns itself on and off and wondering when I can leave without losing face. And I think it might snow.

Anxiety like this sneaks in between thoughts—a ghostly and bitter sinking of the solar plexus. It is sure of itself in a way I am not. It knows that I cannot, that even to try will end in shame, and that I was a fool even to come. "You cannot, you cannot," it repeats. I am afraid.

So I lean into this sinking dread. And as I do, I sense something else here: an openness, a spaciousness. In a way I cannot say, this "something else" is larger than the fearfulness. It is wide, translucent, empty, yet almost a *something*. It is strange and appealing, this whatever-it-is just below my fears, this steadiness. It is kindly, comforting, like a billowing blanket on a tired evening, a gentle velvet warmth in forearms and calves, an effortless waking softness that stretches through my skin, beyond my body, across the room and out the walls into the dusky hillsides in the distance.

And so I sit, this vast empty me beneath this fearful me, much as

I have done for nearly 40 years. This listening, holding, witnessing, vast me is here. It is *who* or perhaps *what* I am. And yet this other me, this worried, scared, laughing me, is also here, astonishingly, miraculously unhealed.

I am closed and afraid. And I am as vast as the colorless air.

I don't know if I am a human being held in the arms of an endlessness, or a vastness having human fears.

Being both these things at once is the peculiar miracle of my life, and of many lives of people on "the path." Learning to live them both, and well, is the challenge.

Waiting for Enlightenment

It wasn't supposed to be like this. When we took up meditation in the early seventies, we all were going to gain enlightenment. It would be life-shattering, the end of all neurosis, clean. It was to be the end of all suffering, *the* revolution of the soul. Enlightenment will, we heard,

> *... put an end to all suffering; filling the heart with happiness brings perfect tranquility to the mind.*[1]

As enlightened beings, we would not be a little happier or just *more* content. Such people are *filled* with happiness. The realized man, the illumined soul... ahhh... he will be steeped in perfect joy. All his desires would be fulfilled, all his suffering at an end.

> *A soul evolved to this cosmic state is eternally contented.*[2]

When we became truly without stress, having utterly relinquished the knots and tensions that had held us in our mundane egos, we would live *eternal freedom in divine consciousness.*[3]

My guru, Maharishi Mahesh Yogi, used to recite some of the Indian texts he had memorized in his youth. Quoting the Hindu *Upanishads*, for example, he assured us that,

> *When [the individual soul] it discovers the Atman*
> *Full of dignity and power,*
> *It is freed from all its suffering.*[4]

> *When a man knows [the infinite], he is free: his sorrows have an end...*[5]

I wanted that. I didn't want to be happier, I wanted perfect happiness. I didn't want less suffering, I wanted to be *utterly* free from suffering. Not fewer but *all* my sorrows should end. I wanted the life Maharishi described: dignified, full of power, helpful to others, deep, suffering-free.

That was the deal. We'd meditate. We'd do our yoga. We'd let go our stresses. We'd work for the TM movement. And we'd gain divine consciousness, full-on perfection, *Enlightenment.* My Buddhist friends were well on the way to *Nirvana.* My Christian friends were going to gain Heaven on Earth. And wouldn't it all be grand?

Dr. Charles Tart, eminently sane scientist of meditation that he is, put it this way. Serious spiritual seekers like me and he himself,

> *[tended] to think of enlightenment as all or none. Somebody is enlightened or somebody is not enlightened.*[6]

And because this was so, to gain enlightenment would be to become perfect.

> *In this all or none model of enlightened functioning... [we think] every single thing an enlightened person does must be perfect.*[7]

Enlightened gurus like Maharishi, Swami Muktananda, Rajneesh or a Zen Roshi like Eido Roshi carried a presence unlike anything most of us westerners had ever encountered. They seemed like god-men. So it was disconcerting to witness, over the years, their feet turning more into clay than we expected: Rolls Royces, sexual dalliances, strange money management, faked miracles, the full catastrophe.

One purportedly realized soul led his followers to stage a bloody gas attack on a Tokyo subway station.

No, enlightenment turned out to be far more ambiguous than the single *summum bonum,* the supreme good, for which I and so many others had been longing.

So here I sit, in just that ambiguity, steeped permanently in some approximation of the openness to which enlightenment points, yet at the same time anxious about the loneliness and the cold and whether I'll have anything worthwhile to say. Whatever this strange both/and life is, it is far more ambiguous than any all or none, or indeed anything I could ever have imagined. I am way too much beast to be a god-man and far too much god to be beast.

Its Context

This strange state of both/and affairs began January 4, 1972, in the Hotel Karina, Mallorca, Spain, at 4:00 in the afternoon. That was the time when the vastness that has no beginning began.

Before that afternoon, I had only known this world: things, thoughts, people, hopes, dreads, loves and losses. After it … well I'm getting ahead of myself.

Mostly being in this world meant being anxious: "generalized anxiety disorder," one doctor called it. "Post adolescent anxiety identity diffusion," said another. To me it was just life.

Anxiety had been with me since before I can remember, which is only about 11. I doubt I even knew the word "anxiety" at eleven. Certainly I didn't know that I was in it, any more than a fish can know it's in water. But it was the ocean in which I swam, every minute, every day.

As I was reasonably successful in high school, it remained in the background. But when I got to the University of Chicago (well-dubbed, "where fun goes to die") I was, for the first time in my life, in a huge class of kids, all of whom were, like me, presidents of their classes and leads in their high school musicals. It's hard to prop yourself up when you're nobody special.

By midway through my second term, I was spiraling into what I can only describe as psychological collapse. The worst part of serious depression is that you can't imagine that it ever was or will be different. It gets harder and harder to hold up your head, to get to class or even to smile, and your life slows into some ever more languorous ennui. By the end of my second term I was pretty much plastered to an orange naugahyde chair in the dorm's windowless TV room, living on vending machine ice cream sandwiches and watching Star Trek reruns till three in the morning.

Towards the end of that first year, I was walking back from the laundry room through the dormitory's moldy basement tunnel. I suddenly heard whispering voices around me. I looked around, but all I saw were dusty corners and peeling overhead pipes. Though I was alone, I heard more and more voices, all at once. Something about being a fraud, about not being who I claimed I was. Ten, twenty, eventually maybe a hundred voices, all unintelligible, all accusing. I've never been so terrified. Lasted about 10 minutes.

About two weeks later the whispers came again. Same laundry room, same basement passageway. Hundreds of voices, all at once this time, terrifying, accusatory, cacophonic.

When they came a third time, this time while I was walking across the quad in a cold late evening's mist, I was afraid I was actually losing my mind. (I was probably right.) So I made my way to the school's mental health clinic, where they assigned me to Myra Leifer, a short Israeli woman. Myra was cute as hell and seemed to genuinely care. Although the whispers came back one only more time, the anxious churning in my belly never abated.

By my third year the churning in my gut had become nearly unbearable. Some unfathomable despondency had taken over my life, as if I was disjunct, living somebody else's life.

The worst of it came on March 15 of my third year. Chicago dyes the Chicago River green for St. Patrick's day, and I found myself sitting on the edge of a rusty I-beam on one of its bridges, staring dizzily down into the green slime below, wondering what it would feel like to hit the water from such a height and whether I would be conscious enough for my swimmer's instincts to take over. No whispering voices this time. No strong emotions. Just curious what it would be like to drown.

I sat on that I-beam for a very long time. Why I didn't jump I don't actually know. But something, some shred of hope or determination or cowardice or life instinct led me to climb down from that beam.

This is something I'm grateful for but will never understand. Even at my most lethargic, something in me just never gave up. (This wasn't true for all of us, by the way. During my third year one of the four of us depressives that sat together in front of the TV till three in the morning actually killed himself.) I have no idea what it was in me that led me to climb off that I-beam and not him.

It was that life instinct, I suppose, that led me into therapy with Myra, to try Zen, to enroll in yoga class and to study a little psychology. None of it seemed to help back then, not really. But that drive to fix whatever the hell was wrong with me, the passion to find a life worth living, to keep going in the face of discouragement and pain, is probably what's kept me going. It's also no doubt what's gotten me to this place, to this book and to the ambiguous spaciousness I feel just now. Despite my anxious and depressive solar plexus that would not abate for 20 years, I never stopped trying.

I didn't have words for it at the time, but during the fall of my senior year I had my first spiritual experience. I used to race my cream colored MGB sports car on back roads outside of Chicago in "motocross" races. One Sunday I was careening at some ungodly speed when all of a sudden, everything else in my life seemed to drop away. All my anxieties, all my thoughts and feelings, even the loneliness just disappeared. For a few moments it was just me, the steering wheel, the hood, and the road. That was probably my first moment of real peace, and at 87 miles an hour no less. And some sort of beacon, as it turned out.

I made it through college by 1969. A college roommate had tried Transcendental Meditation (TM™) and claimed it was giving him some peace of mind. So when I got dumped by one last girlfriend, Lisa, I hitchhiked to Boston to learn it. Hope is a powerful magnet and nothing else was calling me.

I soon found myself standing in my stocking feet in a sweetly incensed room next to one Dan Raney, my TM "initiator," holding an orange I'd found in my sister's fridge and the wilted flowers I had stolen from someone's apartment flowerbox, listening to him chant a strange little song to the gaudy print of a half naked guru on his little altar. He was singing the Sanskrit song not *to* me but *for* me, I felt. The moment felt important, as if this neatly dressed fellow was chanting new possibility.

When he finished we bowed. Then he instructed me to repeat a mantra, a one syllable Sanskrit word, verbally then mentally. Within a few minutes I heard inside what seemed like ten, twenty, eventually perhaps a hundred monks whispering this meaningless syllable right alongside my own mental repetitions, as if they were buttressing my own reedy voice with their gravelly resonance. This was almost as terrifying as those whispers a few years before. But these were singing in unison, and were kindlier, more compassionate and not at all angry. There was something here, I felt: a power, a resonance of love I couldn't have found on my own.

Every time I meditated that week I heard them, with a combination of enchantment, fascination and dread. I'd come out of every meditation drenched. As the week ended though, they just vanished. I've never heard them since. I still don't know who they were or what unclaimed corner of my psyche they'd come from or what they were doing. But perhaps they'd accomplished what they'd come for. Whatever was going on though, those first meditations were certainly intriguing enough to keep me going twice a day, every day.

Within a few months I began to notice odd little effects. My skin would twitch, like a horse might shoo off a fly, more often in meditation than out. I jiggled my legs a little less, I thought, both inside and outside of meditation. My breathing seemed to be slowing down a bit.

About three weeks into meditating, I got summarily canned from an auto mechanic's job. I was just too depressive, I suspect, too low energy. I went home and turned on a Saturday football game (something I *never* do). I had been canned before, but this time, for no obvious reason, I began to cry. In all my adult years, I had wanted to cry, needed desperately to cry. But even with Myra Leifer I had been way too blocked up. But that day, sitting in front of that ridiculous football game, I just wept. I cried, unable sometimes to catch my breath, over the job I couldn't keep. I bawled for all the years and for all the sadness I'd carried without knowing why. I wept for I didn't know what. I'd stop, grab a Kleenex, and then crank up again. I sobbed and stopped, sobbed and stopped for something like an hour and a half.

I felt more cleaned out that evening than I could ever remember. This meditation stuff seemed to be doing *something*!

About two months later, I signed up for my first weekend meditation retreat. Not much seemed to be happening during the weekend, except a lot of time with our eyes closed. But driving home was amazing! The fields and scrub oak barrens seemed welcoming somehow, gracious. It was as if the cranberry bogs and country roads were smiling. For an hour I felt, well, actually happy!

I was hooked. Boring, interesting, tired, energetic or deep, my meditations became the bookends of my daily routine. Like clockwork, twice a day, morning and evening. Haven't missed a day since (egad! 42 years!).

I developed my first real friendships that year. Phil Goldberg, a lanky, funny "Hin-Jew" as he called himself, invited me to play some jazz with him. (We were terrible). I enjoyed my roommate Jussi and his two unbelievably big wolf hounds.

I got (and kept) a job at Strawberry Records, and enjoyed chatting people up about Beethoven and Renaissance madrigals. I got involved there with gorgeous, alto voiced Carol, whose cheeks were hiker-rosy and whose tie dyed skirts swirled when she walked. We'd have long heartfelt talks on breaks from the record shop. I loved to tell her over dinner of my meditation moments and hear of her spiritual insights on her woodsy walks.

But alas, within two days of one of our heart to hearts, I'd need to see her again and feel loved. She must have felt utterly smothered though. Driving her away took about six months this time, which was my longest to date. That I supposed, was progress.

So yeah, there *was* progress in those early days. Within two years of learning TM, I had a few friends, a fairly substantial relationship, a modest job and a steady spiritual path. I'm still not sure just why my life was beginning to take shape, but it was.

Growing up perhaps? Living on my own? The structure of twice daily meditations and the community that came with it? But I'd have to say, there's something about routinely dipping your life into the peculiar dye of inward quiescence, sensing a whole new level of reality there, a whole new possibility for being, that seemed to be helping. You're touching the real in those moments, even if only vaguely, and it matters.

Nonetheless, those old anxieties never lifted, not even for an hour. I still carried that just-this-side-of-weepy feeling. I was still terribly lonely, even when surrounded by crowds of meditators. I was still unsure of who I was, still needy, and still chasing away every woman I'd ever loved. And my churning, belly drooping yet nameless dreads were still with me, constantly.

It was in this discouraged yet hopeful state of soul that I flew to a "TM Teacher Training Course" course, October, 1971, in Mallorca Spain. Which is when it began.

Seeking It

I landed in Mallorca, Spain in October, 1971 and took the movement bus to the thickly carpeted Hotel Karina to begin my nine month "TM Teacher Training" course with crinkly-eyed Maharishi Mahesh Yogi, our short, stringy-haired, much beloved guru.

Maharishi had a *darshan,* a belly-dropping presence, unlike anyone I had ever met. He could be amazingly insightful, attentive, concerned and giggly, sometimes all at once. When he walked into a room, a sandalwood hush would descend over the whole room. The walls would open out and the floor drop away. All 1500 of us (which would eventually become 2500) would stand two deep in snaking devotee lines, waiting to give him a carnation or rose as he walked in, but mostly to get a quick hit of his charisma. He'd look at us with his terrible gaze, or we'd exchange a word or two with him, and we'd walk back to our chairs in a blessed out existential daze. He was that powerful! And he seemed to know each of us better than we knew ourselves.[8]

The evening meetings were mostly Maharishi's lectures. They were rambling affairs at best, long winded at worst. The bolder of us would ask about some theory of stress or about problems in meditation, and he'd answer patiently, if sometimes unintelligibly. He'd talk about how consciousness itself was the "source of thoughts." He'd go over the Hindu theology of formed and unformed Brahman, which was described in the early Hindu scriptures, the Vedas, which were, he occasionally mentioned, some 25,000 years old. Sometimes he'd have a physics professor come up and connect the theory of quantum physics with our meditative depths. Or some psychologist would be invited to make a presentation, and Maharishi would point out parallels between the quantum vacuum state, Carl Jung's collective unconscious, and some passage from the Vedas.

To listen to Maharishi was to listen to nature itself speak. His words and thoughts seemed to be an out-flowing of the way things really are. This little man on his flower strewn dais seemed a fire hose from the source, and we got to stand at the mike and ask it questions. We learned a system as complicated and as thorough as any theology I studied later in graduate school or Theological Seminary, but we were getting it from The Real itself.

Officially we were there to train to become teachers of meditation. And so we did, dutifully. We memorized page after page of teaching material, chanted the long Sanskrit prayer, the *puja,* to each other in small groups, and we practiced the strangely formal ritual movements with our new, shiny brass implements.

Mostly though we meditated. Day after day we sat, eyes closed. Six or eight hours a day, every day, for nine months. We sat alone in our hotel rooms, on floor pillows or leaning against the backboards of our beds. We sat cross legged in chairs or feet down in the Karina's overstuffed love seats. We sat in small groups on hotel terraces and in great lecture halls, eventually 2500 strong.

Our day was divided into "rounds." Thirty minutes of meditation, ten minutes of yoga, ten of the boring breathing exercise called *pranayama*, and maybe another ten to pee or lean against the porch railing, looking out to the windy Mediterranean Sea: that was one round. I generally did my rounds in my hotel room, sitting lotus style in my room's tan love seat, or, against the wall, with legs extended over my richly carpeted floor. For three quarters of a year, seven days a week, I closed my eyes and sat.

For those who haven't spent many hours meditating, it's almost pointless to describe such long term meditation. I can't tell you what others' were like, though my sense is that mine were fairly typical. Some of my meditations were heartbeatingly active. Lots were workaday, with my mind going over to-do lists and plans as if I was at my office desk. But often meditation was like a tender caress, where increasingly slow, languorous thoughts would find their way into a roundness of warmth and softness inside like a purring feline on a warm evening's bed. A gentle kindliness wafts into your forearms and calves, like a waking sleep, and you become very soft with yourself, fighting nothing, seeking nothing, but just letting your mind drift and be awake simply for all the vague, dreamy half-seen thoughts and felt sounds.

To meditate like this is to let go of self. It is to relinquish who you are and to let go of life's concerns into the merest being alive. Such letting go into the smooth presence of simple being is not the kind of visible, salable skill a businessman or a violinist might develop. But it is not at all trivial. To really let go, to *not* try, not even a little, is its own kind of mastery. You learn how to relax over months like those, and to relinquish. You are dropping into the real and it has a quiet but transformative power. I gained the beginnings of the flexibility it takes to self-correct that year. It was the year I discovered what it was to evolve.

Longing for Enlightenment

I am starting to feel a little more confident about being here. I've discovered where the kindling is hidden and where the paper. I have found that when I'm starting the fire, the door likes to be opened a little to let the fire breathe. Though there is still a chill on my neck and calves this morning, I can sense the warmth slowly expanding through the room. It is starting to feel a little like the expanse in my soul that is my reason for being here. I like the settledness I feel here.

There was a longing in the Hotel Karina. I suppose it is the same hunger that has led people to every other TM retreat and probably to every ashram ever. It's not like we tell ourselves in so many words that enlightenment will feel like this or that, though we did speculate about it endlessly that year. The longing for salvation was more like a door we leaned on, expecting it to give way anytime. We were all on the verge of something important, like falling in love or getting into college, only better. For unlike either of them, we were on the cusp of *the* great mystery, and it would be permanent. It was a deep and inexpressible ache—for the perfect life, for more love, for coming alive.

Two thousand five hundred of us on that course, all "just about to fall" into enlightenment. And all looking for portents. One fellow told Maharishi that he often saw streams of colors when his eyes were closed, and then asked if he might be an incarnation of Saraswati, the goddess of art. (Maharishi's kindly and un-cynical answer: "it is a good experience.") My friend Tim was sure he could magically see across the room during his meditations, until someone told him that when he meditated his eyes were half open. We'd repeat rumors of folks who could see divine vibrations in the air or hear celestial music or who had fallen into some sublime state. Tales of "cosmic consciousness" and "unity consciousness" were everywhere.

To be enlightened, Maharishi had assured us, would be to live in harmony with the world around. Everything would go better, all our desires would be met. The enlightened one finds great intelligence, energy, happiness and harmony and, possessed of these, no limit to the fulfillment of desires.[9]

We would become more intelligent, smarter. We would be less self-centered. There would be "no limit to the fulfillment of desires." And it would all come effortlessly.

In his translation of *The Bhagavad Gita*, which many of us read till it was dog eared, Maharishi described *mokṣa*, enlightenment. In it there will be

> *A solid foundation for the actor, and ... the maximum possible success in action with the most glorious fruits.*[10]

We would be solid, impenetrable, unshakable. And with it we'd have the "maximum possible" success in the world. Not just *some* success, mind you, not just *decent* people, but we'd have the *maximum possible* success. Whatever we did or tried to do, the fruits of our efforts would be excellent, wonderful, ticker-tape "glorious."

When one gains enlightenment, Maharishi said, quoting the ninth century Indian philosopher Shankara, when one lives with "the *Atman*" as their consciousness, they would be "ever blissful." They would find, *"the ultimate peace and remain absorbed in the joy which is silence."*

The *ultimate* peace, *the* peace that passes understanding, *the* unchanging, unshaking, immovable peace. The total end of all our anxieties and fears. "Absorbed in", surrounded by, the joy of silence, we would live in a state of

> *"unmingled bliss forever....No matter what [he or she] is doing, the illumined seer ... lives in joy and freedom."*[11]

Bliss at this level would not be ruined by all the complexities and depressions of our everyday lives. We would not be *sort of* blissful or sort of happy. No, to be enlightened was to be simple, joyous, free, untrammeled bliss.

The Beatle's Paul McCartney caught the feel of our hotel in the little ditty he wrote while with Maharishi.

C'mon, Be Cosmically Conscious,
Cosmically Conscious With Me…
Such a Joy, Joy
Such a Joy, Joy
So that Means
Such a Joy

(repeat)[12]

Maharishi wasn't the only guru extolling enlightenment. Buddhism for example describes a similar perfection, the fearless life of *Prajna Paramita* that is "without hindrances."

The bodhisattva depends on Prajna Paramita
And the mind is no hindrance;
without any hindrance no fears exist.
Far apart from every perverted view one dwells in nirvana.[13]

No fears, none. No hindrances. Perfect Nirvana.

Or the Buddhist Lama Lodo:

There will be a spontaneous recognition that the mind which has been meditating on emptiness and the state of emptiness itself are one and the same.[14]

John Welwood saw the same thing among adepts in his Buddhist world: they believed that when they *"have major spiritual openings, they imagined that everything [will] change and that they will never be the same again."*

Sufi Ibn al-'Arabi writes

Then the breakthrough suddenly comes, and with that [spiritual seekers] penetrate their own nature, the nature of others, the nature of sentient beings, the nature of evil passions and of enlightenment ....The great matter of their religious quest is completely and utterly resolved. There is nothing left.[15]

Or the Christian author of The Book of Privy Counseling,

Man's highest perfection is union with God in consummate love, a destiny so high, so pure in itself, and so far beyond human thought that it cannot be known or imagined as it really is.[16]

Virtually every religion or spiritual path holds aloft a heavenly goal of some sort: enlightenment, Olympus, Elysium or paradise, the Muslim's Jannah, Heaven to the Christian or the Jew, Buddhism's Nirvana or the "pure land," Hinduism's *mokṣa* or its s*varga loka,* the center of the universe way up on Mt. Meru. Even dusty, embattled Jerusalem has been a promised land. We all need a promise to keep us going when we get discouraged, I suppose, a far away "there" on which we lean like a door that's about to open.

Like a sunflower reaching towards the sun, I aimed my life towards enlightenment. By the time I flew to Mallorca I was no longer so lost as I had been two years earlier, standing next to Dan Raney holding my little bunch of wilted flowers. But I still longed. For I had tragically little confidence, little sense for who I was or for where I was going and little stability.

Dreads that no one would want to sit with me or jealousy about Judith, my crush of the month, would alternate nearly daily with some euphoric experience or some uplift or about what we would accomplish, only to sink back into depression a day later. Halfway through the year I hung a three by five card on a string from my hotel room ceiling. On one side I wrote, "Today I am up." On the other side, "Today I am down." Every time I would walk in or out of my room I'd give it a little flick. Spinning it—"Up today / down today"—helped me remember at my worst that things would probably change.

No wonder I was longing for enlightenment. It was sanity. It was hope. It was my safe place. It was a way out.

This was the context.

It Enters

It began about two months into the course. It wasn't painful. No dark night of the soul, no burning or shaking. Just that without warning, and so noticeable that I opened my eyes to check them, the palms and the backs of my hands became silent.

Everywhere else I could feel something like faint "pins and needles." Such white noise sensations had always been there, so constant that I had never noticed. But here, on the fronts and backs of both hands, something or someone had suddenly scrubbed my skin super-clean. All the white noise just stopped, utterly.

Absence is an odd sensation. It's more a not than an is. In just that one area, front and back of both hands, I was un-busy. Where low level burbling had been, was now just skin.

By a few days later that strange lack of "noise" had extended itself halfway up my forearms. I felt for awhile as if I was wearing women's formal gloves. By several days later the pins and needles all over my head, face and neck had been scrubbed away. After a few more days the quiet had spread itself over my shoulders and halfway down my chest.

Some otherworldly squeegee was systematically working its way downwards. Utterly silent skin above, slight pins and needles below. Silence was descending down front, sides and back all at once; this quieted layer was slowly and methodically expanding.

This had nothing to do with my ability to feel or touch, mind you. I hadn't become numb. Where the squeegee had done its work, things still felt hard or hot or slippery. I could still hold a hand or scratch my nose. But over half my body, there was now nothing added, no white noise, no sensation beneath the sensations. Just quiet skin.

This newness was not just in meditation, mind you. Walking downstairs to the dining room, listening to Maharishi in the evening meetings, kidding around on the terrace late at night, this strange plane still divided my body into Yin and Yang: quiet silent skin above and noisy below. And with nary a hint of effort from my side to make it so. It just was the new state of my body.

After another week or so, the descending plane halted just above my ankles. I actually kept checking to see if my socks were too tight! But by about a week later, that too had disappeared. Without any fanfare, whatever this was was done. The pins and needles that had until then covered my whole body simply were no longer.

My skin would never again become noisy.

No doubt the enthusiasm for enlightenment with which the course was ripe had led me to attend to this process especially vigilantly. For I expected that when this plane had done its work I'd find myself in some amazing new state of consciousness.

But no. When the plane had finally worked its way out the soles of my feet, my state of consciousness didn't shift. I was actually surprised. Despite the silent epidermis, nothing life changing had happened. Same thoughts. Same snatches of Stones tunes. Same anxieties.

It must have been some meditative blip, I told myself, some "release of stress," which is what we said to each other about meditative experiences when we didn't know what else to say. But except for the quieter skin and whatever slight level of calm that had brought, I just couldn't sense any effects. Mostly it was just odd.

But as I'm thinking back to those days, I'm looking out the bay window at a wintery scene, watching a flock of birds float by, legs dangling awkwardly beneath, the orange beam of the sunrise pointing straight up behind them. Watching them, I am entirely unaware of the surface of my skin. But I am aware how settled I feel as I watch them, how focused and welcoming I am of this moment. It makes me wonder if just a little of the focus I feel doesn't have something to do with that cleansing of 35 years ago and whether without it I would be just that much more distracted for reasons I could never know. I cannot be sure what of today connects to a shift that began back then. But I am settled with the snowfall and the sunrise and the birds and grateful for the ability to welcome them on this crystalline winter's morn.

Ok, back to the story. About a month later, with a sensation so strong that I grabbed at my neck, a tiny tube inside the back of my head suddenly went "zip." And it instantly became silent.

Even after my skin had shifted into quiet, I had never noticed any particular sensations inside my neck. But the moment that bundle of nerves, or whatever it was, zipped itself into silence, I knew that in that area too there had always been faint pins and needles, some understated white noise. I realized it had always been there only when it disappeared.

The cleansing of that little tube had an interesting effect. In some way I can't quite describe, I was able to shift my awareness from looking *at* the spaciousness to standing *within* it. And when I did, I suddenly found myself in some strange and dizzying spaciousness, where my sense of myself now extended noticeably. It, or I, was bottomless and utterly devoid of movement.

With the part of me that could stand outside, I could assign it a place (left side, rear of neck) and a size (perhaps a sixteenth inch by an inch and a half). From within it, it was placeless, directionless, without any obvious boundaries.

Two or three days later during an afternoon meditation, again without warning, a second tiny tube—just to the right of the first—unzipped itself into silence. Again there had always been some pins and needles sensation in that tiny space, and again it instantly and totally vanished.

The only difference between this and the first tube was that when this one disappeared into silence, it seemed to merge utterly with the first. Or perhaps it would be better to say that the first tiny strand now widened to include the second. Wider though it was from the outside, when I shifted my attention to be within it, there was no change in the spaciousness whatsoever.

Except that it may have become just a little easier to shift my attention to be within it, the openness itself was no different.

Standing inside this oddly silent breadth, I still felt a little dizzy, as if I couldn't find my bearings or sense a bottom. It was as if the back of my head contained a wormhole to the infinite.

But only a wormhole. Surreal though it sounds, the rest of me still felt the same. My mind was still full of thoughts. I still worried at dinner that Judith didn't smile at me brightly enough. I still heard snatches of Crosby, Stills and Nash tunes. Yet now at the same time a new and strangely dizzying strand of silence, endlessness.

With that second unzipping the pattern seemed to have set itself. After two or three days, another strand just to the right would *zluuuup* itself down. The bottomlessness would become a little wider (from the outside) and from within become just a little easier to place my attention to be from within it. A few days after that, another tube.

Silence almost disappears upon arrival. The sense of a separate tube or nerve bundle was so quickly absorbed into the expanding width that, except when it was unzipping itself, the next tubule simply disappeared as a distinct zone. Like a raindrop disappearing into the ocean, each tube merged indistinguishably with the widening emptiness.

Every few days another strand would zip off and again merge into the whole. Over weeks a third, then a half, then most of the back of my skull became silent bottomless.

And different. I lived a strangely dual life during those weeks. I continued to think, meditate, hear snatches of Beatles tunes, be taken with how great some girl had looked, write letters.

But now amidst the noise and chatter, there was something new, open and strangely magnetic. It didn't say anything. It didn't give me courage or issue commands. It didn't make my mind still, as I thought enlightenment would. Yet despite its understated simplicity, I couldn't but be terribly aware of it. Something new was here, something spacious, barely sensible and of a nature unlike anything else in my life. And weirdly without end.

The descending plane on my skin had been horizontal. The split here was vertical: silence on the left, activity on the right. In fact it made me a little dizzy. Silence had a lightness to it in comparison to the thinking part, as if it weighed nothing. Going down the stairs I actually tended to list.

This all made even less sense than the changes in my skin, which had made little. Bundles of brain-stem neurons, or whatever they were, unzipping themselves? Into nothingness? And one after another in a slow, nearly mechanical order? The forces that were bringing this about and the systematic widening of this strange whatever-it-wasn't were well beyond anything I could understand at 25. Or at 60 for that matter.

I wish I could say that I was doing something to make these tubes *unzloop* themselves. But from my side all I was doing was sitting in my hotel room and going through my meditation, pranayama and yoga rounds. The couple of years of regular TM, self reflection, retreats, hanging around Maharishi, and committing to be in that room for so many months had no doubt set the stage. Yet lots of very sincere folk in other hotel rooms had done all this and more, and, from the reports then and later, few were undergoing anything quite like this. There's probably some combination of grace and effort involved in these things. But all I knew was that I wasn't making this happen.

I didn't tell anyone about any of this at the time, or for many years. It was all just too … too… weird! This was not some ultimate peace. I hadn't suddenly become some happy or more compassionate camper. From what I could tell, except for this new half-head of silence, I hadn't changed a whit. No, all this was just too confusing, too embarrassingly strange to want to talk about it!

For awhile I actually thought that I was having a stroke. I kept checking in the mirror for facial droop. Or maybe it was something psychological. Probably though, I thought, this was just another of those meditation quirks, "some release of stress," soon to be forgotten.

But on, January 4, 1972, at about 4 in the afternoon, the last little tube on the far right side of my neck zipped itself into extinction. And I've never forgotten.

Becoming It

When that last strand zlooped off and merged into the openness, something did change, and noticeably. Several things in fact. Even if I hadn't been as hyper-vigilant about my inner states as I was, I could not have missed the shift. Who I was, how I thought, how I saw, even how I would sleep from that night on were now, and would remain ever after, different.

What I noticed immediately was that almost all of the background noise in my mind had disappeared. Behind every moment of thinking, seeing or hearing, there had always been other, fainter thoughts, odd snatches of music, hints of feelings, errands I shouldn't forget, half-formed sentences. You know, the monkey mind. Again, I doubt I could have told you before that afternoon, but this chattering brain-hubbub had been constant. Until the moment it wasn't.

Even when the silence was growing but hadn't yet spread across the back of my mind, all these quieter thoughts and feelings had continued to burble along underneath, as if happy for the space in my head to play. They continued even when they only had a tiny corner. But the moment that last little tube merged into the whole, they vanished. Like a newly Zambonied ice rink, too slippery to stand on, my mind became clean, empty. The burbling background chatter simply disappeared.

Oh, I still *thought*. That was the confusing part. Thinking didn't stop. Maharishi had told us about gaining a perfect focus, a mind without any thoughts at all. This clearly wasn't that. And the content didn't change: same girl, something Maharishi had said, a letter home I was writing, when to go for lunch. My mind hadn't shut up.

What did stop was the inarticulate mutterings, the endless half thoughts *beneath* my thinking. It was as if behind the movie of my mind had been scrims behind scrims of thought, dimmer, movies I could barely make out. But that afternoon it was as if the light had suddenly shifted so that the front scrim became opaque and suddenly I was watching just one movie. I was thinking only one thought at a time.

Not perfect quiescence, but much more focused. Whereas before I had been struggling to keep my attention where I wanted, I suddenly was able to put my attention on something and have it pretty much stay there. Oh, I still had to bring the old monkey mind back sometimes. But now I was taming only one monkey, not a herd. It was like getting eye glasses for the mind.

I was disappointed though, of course. Maharishi had assured us of a perfectly silent mind, but I was still thinking.

Though I wouldn't realize it for many years, however, there was a promise in that moment. I only recognized it perhaps 20 years later, when I was a professor at Hunter College. A student asked me a question to which I didn't have a ready answer. I paused, naturally. And while I and the class waited, I realized—with not a little astonishment—that at that moment I was not thinking any thoughts at all. My mind was completely silent. Some sort of planning about what I was to say seemed to be going on. But wherever that was taking place, it wasn't anywhere in my conscious mind. I was aware only of a richly pregnant silence.

After a pause—of normal length, was my sense—the answer came out. I had no idea ahead of time what I was going to say, for my mind had been silent. In fact I heard my answer only when they did. And it wasn't half bad! I've often caught myself scoping something out with this strange way of not thinking, and not knowing ahead of time what I'm going to say. Thoughtless thinking.

But none of this did I know to expect on that January afternoon in Mallorca. All I knew then was that though the background noise had disappeared and I was focusing on one thought at a time, I was still thinking. So this shift could not be the "silent mind of enlightenment" for which I, like all 2500 of us, had been waiting.

A second effect became obvious as that last tube zipped itself off. This one is harder to describe. If you had asked me before that afternoon who or what I, Robert Forman, was, I probably would have pointed to somewhere on my mid chest and said, “I’m here, me, Robert!” I’d be trying to get at some vaguely localized sense of a self that I suspect we all have. I, me, Robert, was in there—somewhere.

But once that last strand fell into silent openness, my sense of who or what I was instantly changed with it. I was now the new bottomlessness. Or rather it, the vast openness, was now *me*.

Strangely enough, there was nothing Robert-ish in this new sense of myself. The bottomlessness had no particularity. It had nothing to do with this particular guy, Robert. What or who I was (and continue to be) became more like an “it.” “It,” the consciousness that beheld whatever I saw, felt or spoke, was now me (boy this is hard to express!). Everything I did, thought about, ate, laughed at, even my anxieties, were now encountered by or from within this strangely endless translucence. “I” was now “It.”

These are deep waters. I’ve been living this way for almost 40 years and I’m still not sure I understand it. Our sense of a self is something we carry or are for all our lives, without really knowing very much about it. We all share some such vague and unlocalized sense of what or who we are, I think, though we can’t quite grasp what that is. But that day my ineffable sense of who or what I am shifted into this weirdly characterless yet infinite openness.

The very idea that we can change something so intimate to who we are, so core, must sound preposterous! Had it not happened to me that afternoon I would never have known it possible. Oh, Maharishi had often described a “change in self” and a “shift in consciousness.” I’d probably said these very words a hundred times. But I had no idea, really, what such phrases meant or what it might feel like. To shift your deep and unsayable sense of a self into some empty fullness? I could never have imagined such a shift before I knew it. And I knew it only because I had become it!

Yet ever since that January day, if someone were to ask me, “who are you, really?” I would now answer quite differently. My sense of who I am actually become much more specific, even precise. No more do I have to point inside to some "vaguely non-localized sense" of a self. What or who I am is now spacious emptiness. Period. I'd touched it occasionally in silent moments in meditation or on walks. But from that day on it became the very me that was wondering about it. I became, and have remained, "It."

What surprised me about this deep change in what I am was that it was so much more modest, so different in kind and quality than anything I could have known to expect. The only thing I could have hoped for was something *in* my world, within my repertoire of experience, I suppose. We just have no way to conceive of anything else. I could only look for what I could imagine, hope for something that answered my longings, cured my wounds or made me happier. But this silence, this shift in who I was, was simply outside my repertoire. It was of a whole different kind and quality than anything I knew. And it came of its own accord.

I discovered a third effect some two days later. I was standing on the triangular porch off my hotel room, looking through the mist at the white caps dotting the Mediterranean. Something about the scene was somehow different. The sea seemed particularly vibrant, the fog vivid. The drizzle against my bare arms felt unusually cool and crisp.

Then it occurred to me: what was different wasn't the scene. It was me. The Mediterranean was so alive, the mist so cool because I was now more alive to them!

Standing on that porch, feeing the chilly January air on my cheeks, unlike where I used to be, I was no longer *in* the scene. Rather I was *holding* it, conscious *of* it, attending *to* it.

Maharishi had talked endlessly about an enigmatic aspect of enlightenment: *sak in or witnessing*. In it, silent consciousness

> *is experienced as wholly* ***separate from activity****...*[17]

> *When the mind is experiencing objects through the senses, he is awake in the* ***awareness of his self as separate*** *from the field of*

experience and action. ... He is awake in the world and awake in himself.[18]

I had always imagined this *sak in,* "witnessing," to be some sort of doubled-up consciousness, as if you'd stand back, arms folded, and make yourself watch yourself. The few times something like this had happened before, I was both looking at something and trying to watch myself look. While I was reading, for example, I'd also imagine myself as if from a few feet away, sensing myself sitting in the chair reading. It sounds, and was, pretty grueling.

But leaning against that cool porch railing, feeling the drizzle on my forearms, was just the opposite. There was no extra work in this experience; witnessing was utterly effortless. Looking over the misty dunes and the white caps, I was simply conscious *that* I was looking, feeling, thinking. I was at once a seeing and a separate, silent awakeness. It was that awakeness that was conscious of all this. And being so terribly conscious at that moment, *witnessing* myself seeing, was astonishingly fresh! I was simply and richly conscious of being there, both looking at the sea and conscious of doing so. How utterly normal! How utterly new!

I was not trying to witness, not even a little. I just was watching it all. And doing so took as little additional effort as it takes to have a right hand. I was just present to the white caps, present to the cool of the porch rail, present to the mist. I was conscious and conscious of being conscious, that's all.

I stood at that porch rail for the longest time, feeling the light rain, watching the clouds rolling in above the churning waves, *sak in.*

I am struck with the *dualism* in what I've just written. Seeing and at the same time *aware of* the seeing. Silent consciousness *plus* active in the world. Absolute *and* relative.

Yet my *experience* didn't become dual. The moment itself — conscious of those whitecaps and of awareness itself — was deliciously integrated.

What had come into play was a newly *dual structure*. Before that time, I experienced all my thoughts, feelings, excitements and whatnot as all jumbled together with who or what I was. I had always been a single changing, moving, intermixed *heap* of processes.[19]

But starting that day, that heap was no longer heaped. I was conscious and I was seeing. And ever since there have been two very distinct *kinds* of things in my every moment: a moving, thinking, feeling, embodied thing, a Robert if you like. And an unmoving, witnessing, unchanging conscious thing, an "It." The seer and the seen, silence and activity, absolute and relative, now structurally distinct. I am dual. And I am effortlessly one.

When the weather cleared the next week, I took my first walk down to the beach. Cumulous clouds caught my eye, billowing white and cottony above the wide curve of the Mediterranean, up and up and behind one another. The billows, the ocean and even the light haze above the water seemed to reach backwards more than I'd ever noticed, as if they'd gotten thicker. The whole scene had a surprising depth to it. When I turned back towards the Karina, one scrawny tree seemed especially in *front* of the next. And the bushes were *behind.* It was like I had put on 3-D glasses.

This was a fourth effect. I've always seen depth like anyone else, I suppose. But this was categorically different. It was as if everything—thick or thin, tall or short, heavy or cumulous-light—had become strangely thickened, more layered. Left, right, up, down, front and behind—each seemed more insistent than they ever had. The world became deep. I liked it.

As I've lived over the years with the changes wrought by that January shift, sometimes I've doubted if anything at all happened. It's become so normal that I have sometimes wondered if I just made all this up. But then I'll find myself on a drive through the Colorado Rockies and be bowled over by the height above height of a rounded forest hilltop. Or I'll drive across New York City's Triboro Bridge and be astonished by the depth of the canyons of glass and steel, and

I cannot possibly miss the visual changes that began that month.

Looking out my window just now, a herd of five deer stand like sculptures in the distance, bending into the snow for the grasses hidden beneath. There is a hill behind them and another behind that. To the left and further back, another mound rises even higher, hills rising and disappearing like breathing abdomens. Through the graying mist I can just make out another one even further back. Patches of green grass peer up through forests of snow, and behind them and on the left, red barns and white farm houses dot the hills. Just above them, jagged clouds hang heavy with snow like gauzy chandeliers, and all beneath the endless canopy of the sky.

I became aware of one final effect about a week after that cumulous walk. I woke up one morning certain that, although I'd clearly been asleep, all of me actually hadn't been. Some odd bit of awareness had persisted through the night, awake. I had been fully asleep, for sure, but not quite, not all of me.

Maharishi often told us that one of the marks of enlightenment would be what he called "wakefulness in sleep." Even though you're asleep, something inside remains conscious.

> *"the transcendent state continues to maintain itself at all times, in a natural manner, irrespective of the different states of waking, dreaming or sleeping."*[20]

You or "it" remains aware of your own consciousness even while sleeping: "Even when it is night for all others," as the Gita put it, you remain wakeful."[21]

Frankly wakefulness in sleep had always sounded pretty awful. Sometimes I had lain half awake all night, worrying about how tired I was going to feel the next day, wondering what I had eaten that had caused such insomnia and thinking maybe I should get up and open the window and … But then I'd get up and feel surprisingly refreshed. The idea that I'd have to go through this every night for the rest of my life sounded positively grueling!

But witnessed sleep that night, and every night since, actually seemed quite natural. I was awake inside, sure, but the wakeful part was so understated, so unobtrusive and natural that there was nothing at all traumatic about it. Even today, I hardly bother to notice whether I was awake inside, unless like last night (when I was writing this section) I have some reason to notice. But it's there, it's how I sleep.

Sometimes it's hard to tell if I've actually slept. Here is another peculiar side effect of all this. Since waking and sleeping are so continuous, to know if I've been asleep I have to check the clock to see how long I've "not been asleep." Weird, but you get used to it.

Strangely enough, this new sleep pattern has turned out to be probably the most useful aspect of the shift. Before that time I used to wake up bleary eyed and fogged over. I'd hit the snooze alarm, wake up, fall asleep and hit the snooze button again. Finally I'd wake up, all groggy and grumpy. But ever since that morning, when it's time to wake up, I'm just awake. There's no bleariness, no snooze button. I'm just awake. I suppose it's because consciousness doesn't have to switch states, since I was never totally out.

The main advantage of this over the years has been that if the phone rings in the middle of the night I can just pick it up and talk. This is not to say I necessarily want to answer some midnight call (like from my daughter's teenage girlfriends). But I can if I choose, for my faculties haven't entirely shut down like they used to. They've gone on something like "pause." Sometimes I've wondered if my kids ever noticed that when they'd call or come home late and whisper something in the door, I'd answer.

Despite all these changes, big and small, and with all the perspective of an impatient 25 year old, all I felt back then was disappointment. My mind hadn't become totally silent, the world hadn't been transformed, and I was still spinning my up/down three by five. I still got nervous before I went downstairs to dinner. I was still afraid I'd never make a decent TM teacher and I was still often lonely. Those tubes and sleep changes were interesting and all, but compared to the end of all suffering for which I was waiting, this was pretty much squat.

Ah the impatience of the young! For sitting here, some 40 years later, these seemingly small changes were the beginning. It was an understated earthquake: for the first time in my life, probably for the first time in the life of anyone in my genetic lineage, I now was thinking only one thing at a time. I was conscious and aware that I was, and without effort. And I now knew myself as an empty, spacious consciousness.

Since that time, whatever this strange and effortless otherness may be, it has seeped into so many byways of my life that even here in my hermitage I'm still discovering its ramifications. It would eventually help me rise like Lazarus out of the tomb of anxiety and fear in which I had been long buried. It would eventually lead me to rethink every choice I had made and every belief I had held. It would call me to recreate every relationship I cared about and to a level I could not have even conceived back then. It would cause me to relinquish nearly everything I had held dear or had known myself to be. And slowly, haltingly, but genuinely, in its shadow I would become freer.

And ever since, while the rest of my mind and life percolates along in its active way, this new piece and structure are just there, steady as you go. I am happy and it's there. I am sad and it's there. I am bicycling or anxious for reasons I do not know, and it's there. It is a strangely steady something in an unsteady life, a candle flame in a blizzard.

Behind everything I do now is this bottomless emptiness, so open as to be without end. I have grown accustomed to the fact that this is now me. Not the me of doing dishes, not the me that is worried or writing a paper, not the me that feels alone or scared or happy. But it is the me that watches and lives and holds it all. I am, strange to say, infinite. And astonishingly, miraculously, the old me is here as well.

A steady vastness like this so remarkable, so unlike the rest of what I can know or be that my life would eventually have to re-form itself around it (or live forever unresolved, bifurcated). Sweet soft water wears down rock cliffs, given long enough, and this empty quiet carries something of such gentle inevitability.

It was neither sweet nor kindly nor angry. It didn't end my loneliness and it didn't make my anxieties go away. It was not a good feeling, except in a very narrow sense. Nor was it painful. It simply was. And is. It has remained humble, quiet and unassuming in almost every way. But it is real and permanent and of a nature I could not and still cannot possibly understand.

You can expect experiences like the ones you've known. You can imagine yourself in a cool breeze in a sunlit lagoon, even when you are not there. You can imagine the smooth warmth of a good massage. But absolute total effortlessness, as permanent and as peaceful when you are still as when you are running, the same whether you are awake or deeply asleep, you simply cannot conceive, not quite. You can imagine something *in* your consciousness, when you are focused and attentive. But a shift *in* that very consciousness, your becoming a permanent bottomlessness that is aware of it all, you simply have no way to imagine, not really. That is, until you *are* it.

With my months and years of meditative practice and of letting go, I had no doubt helped lay the ground for it. Effort, as I've said, clearly played its role. But an unflinching silence like this, real and of a nature so beyond our own, can only come *to* us by grace, not *from* us, not from effort. We simply cannot create that which we cannot imagine. For consciousness at this level must be an outcropping from a *ganz andere*, something wholly other.

As I remember those disappearing strands and the quiet that entered my life those weeks, I am looking out at the burdock pods and thistles, bent under the weight of the snow, glistening in the afternoon light. I find myself welcoming the thistles and stems in a way I doubt I could have long ago, welcoming the pods and the shimmers of blowing snow as if here with me, inside my belly. It is as if I am tuned into the moment with some diaphanous glue and there is no turning away. This world-welcoming has matured over the decades in ways I could not have expected back then. Yet in some quiet way it clearly is the inheritance I have received from the understated gift that began in that love seat so long ago. And I am grateful.

None of this did I know at the time though. I had no idea. All I knew was that this wasn't what I had been pining for, and I was disappointed.

I was looking for spiritual party favors. What I got was an existential earthquake.

Chapter 2

Dismissing Its Illusions

Disillusionment, Part I

A little Buddha sits immovably on the stone wall in front of my hermitage. Yemana, who manages these hermitages and is more Buddhist than anything else, no doubt planted him there. Even with snow on his lap and shoulders, he seems to embody how silence feels inside, and how I feel these days. He is erect, comfortable. His robe hangs effortlessly. There is moss under his arms and knees, bespeaking not age but character. It's his otherworldly steadiness I like, as if he is in the snowy world yet also beyond it.

I would not have recognized him when I left Mallorca, ready to change the world.[22] He was other, theirs, a Buddhist artifact. And Buddhist practices, I knew with all the certainty of the young, were not as fast, not as good.

I also would not have recognized him because I hadn't yet come to terms with the new silence inside. Oh, I knew it was there alright, but I hadn't even begun to understand what it was and what it wasn't.

That process began with my first days back from the retreat as a TM teacher, booking library rooms, putting up posters and giving TM intro talks, and my weekends chanting the mellifluous Puja prayer, muttering mantras, and teaching people the delicate art of not trying. My weeknights I spent in class after class, describing the long term effects of meditation.

But I often felt somewhat disingenuous. Here I was extolling the virtues of meditation and describing the promises of enlightenment, but my own life of non-self, the permanent witness and changed sleep wasn't at all like what I was extolling in lecture after advanced lecture. I still felt awfully fragile. My friendship with Richard, my fellow teacher, never seemed to reach beyond who would offer the weekend's advanced lecture. And though I enjoyed chatting with the itinerant TM teachers who floated in and out of our center, it rarely clicked.

Sometimes I'd actually sit by the telephone during evenings in my apartment, waiting for someone, anyone, to call. I'd make a date or go for a movie or a drink now and again, but my dreads were intense. I was lonely.

It's one thing to be depressed. It's another to be depressed when it challenges the very claims around which you've built your life. How on earth could I be carrying spiritual silence, a permanent cosmic *Atman*, and still be lonely or unhappy or scared? "*A soul evolved to this cosmic state*," Maharishi had assured us (and I was repeating in evening lectures) "*is eternally contented*."[23]

I heard Lisa, my college girlfriend, was around, and made a lunch date with her. I remember wearing a maroon turtleneck and crisp black pants to meet her and feeling sharp and well put together for her. It was good to see her, but alas it was obvious I was still a little desperate. The only thing that reassured me was that I was a *little* desperate, not a lot. Which was, I supposed, progress.

Late in that year, 1972, I met dark eyed, sober and upright Yvonne, a recovering Mennonite and a surprisingly principled soul. She was slender, striking and interesting as hell, but for some reason that damned desperation didn't come up. We hung out for hours and soon became actual friends. Yvonne turned out to be the first woman I could just be with. That really was progress.

But being the urgently confused child I still was within the next few years, I broke it off with her four or five times. Poor her! Every time I did, though, I'd call her to tell her how crummy I was feeling and to see if she was doing alright. She would tell me how much she missed me as well and we'd soon crank it up again, holding hands across the chasm I was still creating. Crude and conflicted though I was, our relationship kept growing. And she was foolish enough to keep hanging out with someone as confused as me.

Not quite lovers and not quite friends was, I suppose, about as much love as I could handle. And it was going longer than anything I'd managed before, I told myself. But it wasn't even close to the overflowing universal blissy love that we'd heard so much about:

> *[In enlightenment] the qualities of the heart have gained their most complete development. Universal love then dominates the heart which begins to overflow with the love of God; the silent ocean of bliss, the silent of ocean of love, begins to rise in waves...*[24]

I was expecting something magical to sweep me, sweep us, off our feet. But this *sure* wasn't how enlightenment had been billed. I was not "free from all my suffering" nor "eternally contented." I wasn't even happy, for God's sake. On the other hand, if what had happened to me wasn't enlightenment, then what on earth was all this witnessing and changed sleep patterns and steady silent consciousness? How could you be established in a permanent silence and be *unhappy* for God's sake?

I'm not sure which was worse, my confusion about the silence in the back of my life or the disappointment with its (lack of) everyday effects.

By January 1973 I could no longer afford the luxury of teaching TM for virtually no income, so I got a job at M.R. Forman and Son, my father's thriving paper and janitorial supply firm. His people wisely started me driving a forklift truck, then managing the warehouse, and eventually doing customer and vendor relations.

Though business was fun in its way and I enjoyed meeting my dad's workaday persona, try as I might I never could remember the catalogue page numbers for the aluminum foil, bundles of 25 pound grocery bags, Ajax Silica Cleanser or this week's price for 12 ounce Styrofoam cups. Though I wrote the customer letters well, I often misfiled the ones I wrote. And that the 333 dispenser napkins cost 12% less than the 334's, or that we were out of both till next

Thursday, was way beyond me. Sometimes I'd walk across the room and forget by the time I got to the other side why I'd come.

These hard-nosed facts presented even more spiritual confusion. Permanent inner silence was supposed to make us able to concentrate and succeed at whatever we did. Enlightenment brings

> *the maximum possible success in action with the most glorious fruits"*[25]

> *"When a man is established in [absolute silence] his activity ... enjoys the full support of all of nature."*[26]

> *"With higher consciousness comes ... the support of nature to fulfill your most cherished desires."*[27]

Yet here I was, established in absolute silence and failing miserably in my own family business. This was *not* what I had bargained for!

I don't want to fall into cynicism here. There really was a depth here that was well beyond what I could have imagined when I began meditation. The waters of spirit were still utterly translucent and unlike anything I knew when I begin all this. Yet it certainly was not the panacea we had been promised and for which I had been pining. I think Maharishi was indeed describing a real and significant life shift. There really is enlightenment. But whatever had shifted in me was almost nothing like he had made out, or as one sided, or as pleasant.

In retrospect, maybe the problem was me. I was awfully neurotic at 25. I had begun meditation just emerging from chronic depression. I was still dealing with constant anxiety. Maybe I was just too screwed up for silence to realize its promise. Yet on the other hand, I probably wasn't all *that* different than the others on my retreat.

The conundrum with which I was struggling may have been bigger and more important than my personal neurotic vexations.

Finding your life's work in a complex context like ours is something that our Indian teachers may not have had to confront. In India, a man typically did what his father did. So too a woman. But I'm an American, and the albatross was around my neck to discover a life's task that was "right for me." What I am to believe, who I am to wed, what I am to do — these too were my choices, not my religion's, not my caste's and not my parents', and terribly complex. Perhaps closing your eyes or gaining inner quiet is just not particularly well-suited to answer such multivalent life questions. Perhaps I was looking for too much from a shift in consciousness.

But I get ahead of myself. All I knew in those days was that I was frustrated and disappointed with the idea of enlightenment, and that I was tired of my confusions and my anxieties.

So by 1975, after three years with super-clean skin and unzipped neck tubes and bottomless consciousness behind all my thoughts, I was struggling in my father's business. I was still anxious, constantly, lonely often and sometimes downright depressed. I was screwing up my relationship with Yvonne. How on earth could such a life be anything like the enlightenment we had heard so much about? Whatever this new state might be, "*eternal freedom in divine consciousness*"[28] this wasn't!

So, finally, I gave up. It was time, I told myself, to stop asking my infernal question. It was time to stop debating with myself, wondering what this was or wasn't. A steady silence underneath thought and perception, a new sense of self, an openness while I slept, was nice and all. But it was just too … too… underwhelming. This just couldn't be that much vaunted *mokṣa, nirvana,* enlightenment.

And so with a deliberate and determined vow, I stopped asking the damned question. And I put the whole matter out of my mind.

Or so I thought.

Full Catastrophe Disillusionment

There is a freedom in the air this morning. The hermitage feels comfortingly wide. Heat is coming off the grate, silently unfurling itself like a healing fog into the corners and dust balls and crevices. And there is space here, warm, open, soft.

I learned many sacred words in graduate school—words like Brahman or God or Allah or Enlightenment or even self-effacing sacred words like Tao or *Shunyata* (emptiness). But I can think none of these into this softness. I know I can use them to describe what is here this morning. But they just don't stick. If I try to affix one of them — say Brahman — to the space and warmth I feel, my jaw tightens and the spaciousness swirls and ossifies around it, like a grain of sand in an oyster. It is easy to mistake words like Brahman or God or the Tao for the vastness. But they have no home here.

There *is* a kind of certainty in this spaciousness, but it's not one that can be spoken. The certainty here is of being.

The irony is, I wouldn't know this if I hadn't learned words like Brahman or God or *Shunyata*. To begin, to stay with and even to master the territory, you need to learn core ideas, key words, maps. Key terms must be part of any spiritual or religious life. But then you need to let them go.

When I was a true believer, I knew the right words. I knew the right way to think. I knew to meditate the fastest way (thus the *best* way, of course!). I knew to not force. I knew how to talk the talk: I spoke, we all spoke, in soft voices; we wiggled our fingers just so when we talked, much the way Maharishi did. We knew the real and true goal. We knew the right way to eat, vegetarian, heavy on the bulgur, light on the cheese. We knew that anyone's troubles—well, everyone's actually—could be answered by getting rid of stress, and we knew that they could "reduce stress by meditating, using a scientifically verified technique."

The TM movement was also community. It was hundreds or thousands of people with whom I could have coffee and assume they'd pretty much get my life, my cynicisms, my hopes. It was "us" in a world that saw us as a little weird or threatening. TM was my life-world.

Despite its foibles and gossip and garish bazaar-poster colors and the stifling of doubts that seem to come with any group-think, the TM movement was home. It gave me a footing in what was true and meaningful, and in it I found a purpose. I was accepted there, probably for the first time in my life. It was friends and commitment and hours of practice and sincere hopes, all offered up to me like a rose. And it was in its womb that the silence erupted into my life.

Because it was all this and more, falling away was probably inevitable.

Doing so began with a simple question that came up in a meditation: "I've been Maharishi's squawk-box for all these years. I wonder what *I* have to say?"

There was no anger in my question. I hadn't been betrayed. I didn't doubt the teachings, didn't struggle with some grand hypocrisy. I just wondered what I might have to offer, what might be on the other side of the mountain.

I'm not sure why it came up just then though. Perhaps the movement had parented me enough. After all, by 1976, a half decade since beginning meditation I'd learned how to wear a tie. I was now eating reasonably healthy. I'd learned the basics of how to teach. I had even conquered the worst of my terrors of commitment and married Yvonne, one of the wiser things I did (and for her one of the more foolish). I had also developed a few solid male friendships. I had gone from being a lost, confused, pot smoking, lonely and occasionally suicidal kid to becoming a contributing member of society, now dedicated to something beyond himself.

The TM movement was a warm home in the blizzard that was my young life. I still miss it terribly sometimes. If it weren't for the inevitable group-think, I'd rejoin it again in a heartbeat. But it was time to leave the nest.

And I doubt I'd be quite as open to the space and the warmth and the simplicity I sense around me at this moment had I stayed.

At first I tried woodworking. I became a reporter for a university paper. I wrote short stories. Then I tried college again for a few terms and actually liked it. Within a couple of years I found my way to the dusty, wainscoted hallways of Columbia University's Department of Comparative Religions to get a Ph.D. in Hindu thought and the nature of religious experiences.

During my second week at Columbia, my charming and obviously knowledgeable Hinduism teacher, Dr. Brereton, mentioned almost in passing that the Hindu Vedas were composed between roughly 1200 BCE and 800 BCE. I raised my hand: "I heard that they were composed 25,000 years ago." And this kindly man who stood at this end of a long chain of archeologists, linguistic and military historians behind him, this humble Ph.D. who knew a fair amount about pre-history and Indo-European migration across the Russian steppes and carbon dating and the early history of Assyria and China and Greece and early military technology, this intelligent man looked at me with the arched brows of someone who has just heard something entirely off his historian's map. "No," he said simply, "that would be waaaay too early."

And there it was. At this point I find the 25,000 year figure to be downright laughable. But it had to be something. My two worlds would inevitably collide. Maharishi had probably stressed the date of the Vedas in part to assure us of their status as the earliest and truest wisdom. But that was *waaaay* too early.

That made him waaaay wrong. How then could I still believe everything he had said? When he missed a simple date by so much, how could I regard him as nature herself speaking? Or perhaps Dr. Brereton was way off? But he was a scholar, a scientific historian. And he seemed so… so… reasonable.

That was the first shoe. The second dropped the next semester in a class called "Religious Language," taught by a lanky and brilliant philosopher of religion, Wayne Proudfoot. Every religious or spiritual system, Proudfoot taught, makes up (or adopts from forbearers) a picture of what there is in the world: good and evil, God and the Devil, Brahman and ignorance, Mara and Buddha-nature. It makes up such a world-view (its *weltanschauung) and* invents a few key terms to describe the key elements of this world-picture — sin, Atman, prophet, Buddha-Mind, messiah, Wu Wei, what have you.

And based on its version of what there is in the world, each religion goes on to make up how one should live in such a world, its so-called *ethos*. It declares that you should believe or meditate or do social action or submit or what have you.

Together these two—what there is and what we should do, along with the great web of words and activities and hopes and foibles to which they give rise — is called a "system of meaning" or, for short, a "language game." A language game is the totality of beliefs, rituals, assumptions, attitudes, feelings, actions and foolishnesses within which some group's people build their lives. Every system, of meaning — be it religious, cultural, political, scientific — states what there is in the cosmos, asks its questions about how we can live in such a world, and then provides the answers. In a kind of theological sleight of hand, every system, every religion, names the real, asks the questions, then answers them.

Christianity, for example, posits that there is something in the world called "sin." Then it asks, "how can we cure sin?" "Well," it says, answering its own question, "do the sacraments or have faith in Jesus or some such." It posits the claim (there is sin), frames the question (how to overcome sin?), then supplies the answer (faith or sacrament). Neat trick, huh?

Hinduism teaches that there is a cycle of birth, death and rebirth: *samsara*. Then it asks, how can we get off that nasty samsaric mouse wheel? "Well," comes the answer, "meditation, devotion, yoga or some such practice. Do one of these and come to the supreme state, enlightenment. Then you'll escape from the cycle of samsara." Again, it describes the world, poses the question and then supplies the answer.

Going to church, getting baptized and even taking tuna casserole to a Sunday Church supper are all part of living within a Christian meaning world. Visiting a Hindu temple, sweets in hand, meditating, singing *bhajans*, eating vegetarian and taking off your sandals at the door are all part of living in a Hindu religious system.

We all do this, was Proudfoot's point. Whether we're communists, scientists, Christian fundamentalists or a political liberals or conservatives, each of our systems asks and answers its own questions, and we live square in the middle of our chosen systems. Even atheists do, who live rather vociferously in a world of "not that, not that." All of us.

Professor Proudfoot never mentioned TM. I doubt he even knew I meditated. But I found his analysis devastating. I couldn't deny that I had grown up in a system of meaning. TM, the TM movement, Maharishi, and the term "stress release"—these were all part of my "web of thought and action." Indeed I saw my problems in terms of the knots and tensions in my shoulders, the physiological "armoring" of stress. And I answered the question about how to heal stress that I myself had accepted with "the deep rest of Transcendental Meditation." My quieter mind and more relaxed shoulders were my signs that verified that it was working. And I had adopted these questions and marks from Maharishi, from my friends, from the movement. I had adopted a picture of the world. Then I had climbed into it.[29]

Every morning meditation, every neck-strand of silence, everything I had believed to be true or important were all part of a system I myself had taken up, entered into and lived within. TM wasn't "the" truth. My meditation wasn't "the" best. It was just a system, one among many, the one I'd lived. What had seemed ultimate truth only weeks before now became demoted into a *context*, my "way to ask questions and then answer them." My life flipped overnight from something real into a self-concocted joke.

I suppose that if I was going to grow up, at some point I would have to let go of the fiction of omniscience — that my way, my system of beliefs or my group was the only true one. Inevitably I would have to climb over the mountain next to my valley.

Inevitable maybe. But devastating. Not only did I come to see that my own TM world was incurably self referential and not the only truth. But now I saw that every system of truth, every belief whatsoever was also self-referential. His course, and the post modernism for which it was a stalking horse, challenged every single claim to truth. This whole postmodernist story put me in a hole I, and our culture, are still climbing out of.

The irony, again, is that we need systems like mine. Had I not learned to pick up the mantra, had I not learned words like Brahman or stress, or even had I not accepted that the Vedas were 25,000 years old, I would not be here. I would never have continued all those years, not had a map, and not have been confronted with silence in the soul.

Yet nor would I be quite so available this morning, quite so free from my own certainties and shibboleths. The post modern conundrum conceals an unseen spiritual gift. It is that *all* words, *all* systems, *all* beliefs are the Tao that can be spoken. The hidden lesson of post modernism is that we can and should let go that which can be spoken. We can release the hold of all our certainties, all our systems.

I would not be as available this morning to the majestic silence around me, this certainty beyond words, had I not learned to relinquish my truths.

But this I didn't know then. All I knew that semester, and for several years thereafter, was that confronting the contextual nature of my own life was painful as hell. The summer after I took "Religious Language" I went for a one month meditation retreat at a TM ashram in Iowa. I tried to explain to Frank and Suzanne and Fred that TM was only answering the questions it had asked, and that TM was just one path of many. I tried to show them with all the puppy-dog enthusiasm of a new convert to post modernism how TM offers a good "map" of reality, but that it is not the *only* one.

That's what I told them. But what they heard me say was that TM was *false*, that *other* paths were *better* and that Maharishi was the *devil*.

To them, their hearts sold out, as we called it, to TM and blissfully certain about Maharishi's wisdom and meditation's efficacy, I had gone over to the dark side. I lost almost every friend I had.

A kind of myopia develops in movements like TM. The confrontation with mystery ends up in confidence, ambiguity becomes certainty. And we become terrified of losing both.

I understand this. We must build our beliefs and cling to our truths. This is essential in the process, I think. But if we are to be free, really free, we must extricate ourselves from our comfortable wombs of truth. For they can eventually become our prisons.

In this day and age, with so many systems of meaning, so many world views, we no longer have the luxury of fooling ourselves with the fiction of our religion's omniscience. Today's ways of thinking and knowing are just too diverse, our books too many, to keep any system's blinders on permanently. Hop on any city bus, cruise around the world-wide-web, watch international TV, go to a Euro-bar. We strive for inner transformation with a Maharishi, learn history from a Professor Brereton, meditate or pray Buddhist style, attend a wedding in a Christian church or a Muslim courtyard, and then go to a scientific doctor to mend our strep throat.

If you read Hindu and Jewish and Daoist and Shaman texts, if you meditate a few times like a Kabbalist or a Buddhist, if just open yourself to an historian like Dr. Brereton or some deep voiced scientist, you cannot help but sense, deep in your bones, that no one of these ways is the full truth, and that no one is fully wrong. You cannot help but eventually reach a point that you can no longer pray comfortably at any alter that sees itself as the only true one.

Our world's pluralism has become too obvious. We can no longer squint our eyes shut to them all. At some point relinquishment of your beloved truth is probably the only sane response.

Disillusionment with our system of belief, with all systems, gets a bum rap. If we face facts courageously, we must recognize that our world is too multifarious, too quilted, for any one system to be final, complete or the only. And scary though this is, it is profoundly freeing.

I've often wondered why a system like Advaita Vedanta or Bhakti Yoga or Pure Land Buddhism that worked so well for folks in India just doesn't seem to be quite enough for us westerners. Or why ancient systems like Paul's Christianity or Muhammad's Islam or even more recent systems like Methodism and Reform Judaism don't seem to work so well for us modern urbanites. Perhaps this is part of it, this confrontation with multi-cultural post modernism.

Transportation being what it was, most of our great teachers — from Jesus to Buddha to Lao Tzu to Luther to Shankara to Maimonides — grew up with people more or less like them. They hung around with people who wore the orange robes or the yarmulkes prescribed by their cultures. Most were acquainted with one, two or at most three cultures (think Jesus's Israel at the confluence of the Jewish, Greek and Roman worlds, or Muhammad's Mecca where Bedouin culture was interacting with Christianity and Judaism). The greatest teachers probably mixed with people of different faiths or castes or systems and led their contemporaries to re-imagine their assumed truths.[30] But in their time they could no doubt assume an enormous number of shared beliefs — that there are god or gods, that some sort of meditation or practice is required, that there is samsara and reincarnation, and thus not have to challenge the process as a whole.

What is different today is that we have access to all of human knowledge at once, and with it confront the very process that they all must use to create meaning and worldview and system. To see through our creation of meaning is no doubt much the same illusion-busting process that a Lao Tzu or a Plotinus might have taught to see through their own shibboleths and assumptions. But doing so in today's context is far more far all-encompassing, deep and devastating.

Traditions are important. We are what we are in part because we learned to meditate or pray or do Tai Chi, and because we learned so much at the feet of our rabbis, roshis or mullahs. We stand on the shoulders of great thinkers, great traditions.

But to grow up in today's post-modern world calls for letting go of the whole systems of thoughts, letting go the entire language-system very fictions that we need to bring ourselves of age. It calls for encountering the wonderful, terrible fact of other ways of feeling and thinking than our favorites. And that, yes Virginia, we made it all up.

I am grounded because I had a tradition. I know the silence beyond sensation because I did. But I can recognize the same erect calm in the Buddha outside my window because I have let it go.

Chapter 3

This is 

Locus Classicus.

So there I was, having survived my first year of graduate school, having come to terms with the self-concocted nature of my own perceptions and the uncertainty of my certainties. And there I was as well, having long ago ceased questioning what had begun that January 4th, some seven years prior. I had let go of my fantasies about the perfect life it was to produce and how meditation would make it all better.

But the silence I feel in my shoulders and through the window this morning has an insistence to it I didn't expect. It would have none of that doubting or wondering or forgetting or remembering. It was simply oblivious to my doubt and queries and, for that matter, my ignoring it. Silence just remained. Whether I noticed or cared or asked about it, it just kept on. Gentle, humble, present and real.

But by my second year in graduate school, 1979, the expansion had expanded quite a bit. What had begun as a thin strip across the back of my neck had thickened to now fill roughly the back half of my head. I was too busy with school and money worries and marriage and life to pay it much mind, but it was there, still, silent a faint and steady worm hole behind my ears to infinity.

So when I read in class after class endless accounts of life changing mystical transformations and of enlightenment, it was only natural to compare—even if only half consciously in the beginning—what these ancient texts were describing with what had been with me for nearly a decade.

In the a-systematic and serendipitous way discoveries like these always happen, I began to hear a strangely consistent but unexpected melody wafting out from between the lines of the classics of the spiritual life. And it was same deep thrum that had haunted and confused me for so many years.

Hindu Enlightenment

The first religion I happened to study was Hinduism, in a course taught by the Professor Brereton whose remark on the Vedas had so unnerved me. I was sitting in the far end of the Columbia Library reading room, looking over the little book he had assigned, *The Vivekachudamani, The Crest Jewel of Discrimination*, by the famous 9th Century Hindu philosopher, Shankara, when I grunted right out loud:

> *The knower of the Atman does not identify himself with his body. He rests within it, as if within a carriage. ... He bears no outward mark of a holy man.*[31]

A "knower of Atman." Strange phrase. He or she is someone who knows the quiet inward awareness, the sense of "I am," within. Atman is sometimes translated as "soul," but it is less personal than the western term. It's more like awakeness or mere consciousness. And after the shifting, we come to know it, or rather be it. It somehow becomes our core sense of what we are.

Shankara was saying that one who knows Atman, this silent consciousness, experiences himself as resting within himself, "as if within a carriage." One senses oneself to be something inside that is of a different kind and quality than anything of the outward body or thinking mind. One comes to sense oneself to be, says Shankara, as if "riding within" the body. To know Atman, in other words, is to sense oneself as *within and separate from* one's thoughts and physical body.

This is what made me grunt out loud: "Oh my God," I realized, "that's just what happened to me!" Silent consciousness had indeed established itself inside. It had become the core of who or what I am. And it did seem to be as if "riding in" my body, and of a whole different kind or quality. What I am, that new sense of "me" that had dawned half a decade earlier, had become in some sense *other*. It, Atman, consciousness, was not "identified with" my body or personality, as he wrote, but more some unmoving sense of "I am," a fullness *within* the body. In but not of. I would never have used such clumsy jargon (but of course I'm not a Hindu philosopher). Nonetheless using Shankara's language, I seemed to have become a "knower of Atman," and like a silent passenger in a carriage.

It was the second line that really got me though: the enlightened "bears no outward mark of a holy man." I had vaguely expected from Maharishi and Yogananda and the hagiographies of the Buddha that an enlightened man would automatically give rise to the kind of belly-dropping awe that led us to stand up whenever Maharishi walked into a room.

But no, a knower of Atman "bears no external marks." He or she won't necessarily talk, walk or look the part. They won't necessarily be happy or good at their father's business. They might not be able to keep a relationship or a marriage going particularly well. And they won't glow in the dark.

Could one even be anxious? Depressed? Even lonely? "No outward marks" could be anything, anyone. It's nothing special. He'd be just a guy, like any other guy, who happens to know himself to be Atman inside. As if riding in a carriage.

After I read this I tracked back in history and soon stumbled across this passage from the earlier and much beloved *Mundaka Upanishad*:

Two birds,
Inseparable companions,
Perch on the same tree.
One eats the fruit,
The other looks on.
The first bird is our individual self,
Feeding on the pleasures and pains of this world;

The other is the universal Self,
Silently witnessing all.

Here it was again, absolute and relative. One who knows "the universal self" is like being two "birds" at once: one pecks noisily and flutters about, the other just looks on. Whatever this sort of person does or thinks, the first bird, active and noisy, is "silently witnessed" by that second bird, the quiet "Self." That Atman bird, which I understood as mere consciousness, is simply aware of whatever that first bird does, thinks or feels. Nothing flashy, paranormal, awe inspiring or necessarily happy; the second bird witnesses pleasures *and* pains.

Well, I thought, that's me too. The silence had indeed established itself in my skull and was "behind" — and witnessing — everything I did or said. The witnessing part was, like these, doing nothing, beholding everything, just conscious. Two birds indeed: an eating, feeling and whistling bird and I was a witnessing one. I was living the Upanishad's existential duality!

Of course, I'd never use such a self-aggrandizing term as the "universal self." But, I found myself thinking, if I put my attention solely on the silence inside, maybe it is in a way "universal." Whatever I say, think or do is connected with me, Robert. But nothing about the inner silence is specifically Robert-ish. It's more characterless, personality-less, like an "it." In the sense that it's not connected with me personally, I thought, I guess it is kind of "universal."

Hardly the stuff of great mythology, but still…

Another passage a few pages later in the *Upanishads* struck me:

Yet when the mind becomes clear,
And the heart becomes pure,
Then can the Self be known
And those who know it enjoy eternity.[32]

I sure as hell wasn't "enjoying eternity." Yet if I put my attention only within the interior silence, this again was weirdly accurate. The interior vastness was, after all, utterly unchanging. What had dawned in 1972 was precisely the same spaciousness that was still with me in 1979, except it had now expanded into more of my cranium. In itself it was the same dizzying bottomlessness, utterly without movement. Consciousness itself was without movement or change. Perhaps I was "enjoying eternity." Not quite the "joy, joy, joy" I had been after, and yet …

In other words, if I dropped the grandiosity of what I'd heard from Maharishi and other gurus, these ancient texts were describing quite accurately what had begun in me half a decade before. Consciousness was riding in the body, witnessing. I lived a twin-bird duality of consciousness and activity, seer and seen.

If Shankara was right and there are no outward marks to this sort of thing, then my earlier fantasies that that such a change would make me successful or happy or thin were all wet. These texts weren't describing personality transplants. They weren't chronicling a perfect life, joy in the everyday or smaller waistlines. They were describing a new structure. Drop the glorious exaltations, drop the flashy outward marks, and what I was encountering in text after text was humbler and more precise: a shift, a newly dualistic structure, *in the relationship between consciousness and its content*. Which was, strangely, just what I was experiencing.

Buddhist Enlightenment

The second religion I studied was Buddhism, in a course taught by the avuncular Fred Underwood. Professor Underwood was one of the best teachers I had at Columbia, but alas would soon be denied tenure (whether for his failure to publish or his outrageously droll sense of humor was a matter of hot debate).

The Buddhist word for enlightenment is probably the most famous of them all: *Nirvana.* It comes from the Sanskrit roots *nir* + √ *vā*, Underwood taught: to cease blowing, to blow out, to become extinguished.[33] It is "the highest and ultimate goal of Buddhist aspirations, the end of all suffering and misery."[34]

When I first heard this definition, "Nirvana" seemed to be denying the world. In it the world seemed to be "blown out." But, I soon came to see, Buddhism defines all its key terms in an opposite way than did the Hindu teachers I had read and heard.

For example, Buddhism's word for consciousness, *vijnana,* doesn't point to some *persistent* awakeness or awareness, as Maharishi and Shankara had used such terms. Rather to be conscious, *vijnana* style, has to do with being aware *of* or *connected* with mental content. Being *vijnana* includes being involved with the window, the stove, these words. So when someone stops or "blows out" consciousness in Nirvana, he or she stops *clinging* to thoughts, sensations or the outward world in the old way. Awareness itself doesn't stop in *Nirvana*; one doesn't go entirely blank. One certainly doesn't die! What gets blown out is the felt-*connection* with one's thoughts, feelings, etc.

I saw this clearly in the Diamond Sutra, one of the most revered Buddhist texts.[35]

In enlightenment, it says, one stops "allowing the mind to depend upon notions evoked by the sensible world (44-45)." That is to say, thoughts don't cease. Rather one stops the *vijnana* process of "depending" on what one sees, smells touches. Thoughts or perceptions happen, but I don't "depend on" or "cling to" (*trsna)* them. That leaves one *separate from* content.

Similarly, "the mind is kept independent of any thoughts which arise within it. (45)" One is *independent* of, disconnected from, unattached to whatever one thinks or sees. We have thoughts and yet somehow remain aloof from them, independent of our thinking. Dare I say witnessing?

Such people, the Diamond Sutra goes on to say, don't cherish "the idea of an ego-entity, a personality, a being, or a separated individuality (31)." If some meditator student did hold onto the sense of a separate self, "he would necessarily partake of the idea of an ego-entity, a personality, a being, or a separated individuality." If I sensed myself to be such a separate personal self, I'd be involved with, attached to, it. I'd depend on it. (35) So in Nirvana one gains "freedom from separate personal selfhood." (62)

This is not to say that the enlightened being ends up without a personality. He or she will still be funny, thoughtful, foolish or stubborn. We don't cease having characteristics, personalities.

What we can do, and this seems the point, is to stop "cherishing," i.e. being caught up in, our personalities, our bodies, our egos. We can come to sense ourselves as separated from these, sense our bodies and personalities as "out there" as it were, or as "not connected with" that which we know ourselves to be (as if riding in a carriage). We can pull ourselves away from the fiction of "me," in other words, and hold the personality and ego as unconnected with what we are inside. We come to be alone and quiet:

> *Who sees Me by form,*
> *Who seeks Me in sound,*
> *Perverted are his footsteps upon the Way*. (65)

This "Me" we're after is not found in form nor heard in sound. It is beyond them all.

In other words, what we have in enlightenment, Buddhist style, is a shift in the structure of the human being. The sense of ego, personality and sensations come to be encountered as unconnected with that non-form, non-thought quiescence that one senses inside. To blow out *vijnana,* to disconnect from the thoughts and activity on which I have depended, is to blow out (or separate ourselves *from)* the content of our minds. What we blow out is not awareness in itself, but the seemingly inevitable linkage with whatever we see or feel.

To describe the quiescence one encounters inside, Buddhism offers another famous term, "*shunyata*." The enlightened one is said to be or know *shunyata (*emptiness). This is based on the image of something that's "blown up," like a balloon, and as if empty on the inside. Again *shunyata* at first seemed to be world-denying, pointing to some lack, some emptying out. But no. It's describing what it is to be awake and un-attached inside. One becomes *empty* of content, empty of particulars: *shunyata*.

"Jeez-oo-wiz," I realized, "it's the same damn thing that Hinduism is describing as fullness." Someone in the state of *Nirvana* knows that which is awake but removed from ego as *shunyata*. The Hindus call it fullness. But in the end are a contentless fullness and a full emptiness really that different?

The more comfortable I've become with Buddhist language, by the way, the more I've come to prefer the term *shunyata,* "emptiness" over "Brahman" or "Christ Consciousness" or even my vaguely Hindu term, "bottomlessness." For the sense of spacious silence that whispers itself through my body, into the room and out through the windows, walls and hills outside is, in itself, empty of content. "S*hunyata,"* an emptiness, seems to catch this well. An empty fullness perhaps?

Ancient Buddhist texts like the Diamond Sutra are awfully grand. They're great teaching tools. Yet the more I've read them, the more convinced I've become that the transformation they're describing is much the same as the Upanishads', Shankara's and, yes, my own. Can we have been overblowing enlightenment to this extent? Can it be that a modest yet permanent shift in the structure of consciousness is pretty much what those wizened old sages were after, and that such shifts aren't peculiar to any one religion or meditation program? Can it be this simple?

Christianity

A course in Christian mysticism came next, taught at Barnard College by a diminutive but energetic Professor Parham. She was pinch hitting that semester, and was hardly an expert. But she introduced me to several wonderful figures, one of whom I soon wrote a book about: *Meister Eckhart, Mystic as Theologian* (if you can forgive the plug).[36]

I certainly had never expected to see enlightenment described so well by some westerner, much less a medieval Christian friar.[37] Nonetheless despite Meister Eckhart's antique imagery, I found myself swimming once again in familiar waters:

> *The soul has two eyes, one inward and one outward. The soul's inner eye is that which sees into being ... The soul's outer eye is that which is turned towards all creatures...through the powers.*[38]

"The soul has two eyes." One of them points outside. With this outward orientation we see, touch, move around, etc. Sometimes Eckhart calls this worldly side our "outer man" or "outer powers." The other "eye" "sees into being." Turned inwards, this one beholds what we are at our depths.

Sound like the Upanishad's two birds to you too? "Something" inside—he sometimes calls it a spark of the infinite—witnesses all our activities and perception. Something unchanging is separate from and attentive to that which is changing.

Eckhart describes such a state as analogous to a "door and a hinge." Think of some thick medieval wooden door swinging open and shut. That's like out outer man; we move and talk and swing around. But the hinge pin holds the door to the wall. Like our "inward man," it doesn't move. It "remains immovable." Like the Upanishad's second bird, something active is held by something still and detached. Here's the whole passage:

> *However much our Lady [The Virgin Mary] lamented and whatever other things she said, she was always in her inmost heart in immovable detachment. Let us take an analogy of this. A door opens and shuts on a hinge. Now if I compare the outer boards of the door with the outward man, I can compare the hinge with the inward man. When the door opens or closes the*

> *outer boards move to and fro, but the hinge remains immovable in one place and it is not changed at all as a result.*[39]

Here again is a revered thinker depicting a significantly different structure of awareness. He calls such a transformed life "the *geburt (*birth*)* of the son in the soul." An active, worldly man is outside, as it were, alongside something silent, unmoving and inner. This inwardness is the "son in the soul." Here again is the the very dualism that had confounded me for so long.

I found hints of something similar in *The Cloud of Unknowing* and St. Theresa's *Interior Castle.* But the book that sealed the deal was the last we read that term: Bernadette Roberts's *The Experience of No Self.*[40] Perhaps because she shares my modern sense of autobiography, or maybe because she didn't spin it much, her memoir was the *piece de resistance.*

Bernadette was an ex- Christian nun, a mother and a housewife. She had regularly gone to a local chapel to meditate. On previous occasions, she wrote,

> *. . . I had come upon a pervasive silence of the faculties so total as to give rise to subtle apprehensions of fear. It was a fear of being engulfed forever, of being lost, annihilated or blacking out and, possibly, never returning. . . .*

But on one particular afternoon, as she was concluding a meditation,

> *once again there was a pervasive silence and once again I waited for the onset of fear to break it up. But this time the fear never came. . . . Within, all was still, silent and motionless. In the stillness, I was not aware of the moment when the fear and tension of waiting had left. Still I continued to wait for a movement not of myself and when no movement came, I simply remained in a great stillness. . . . Once outside, I fully expected to return to my ordinary energies and thinking mind, but this day*

I had a difficult time because I was continually falling back into the great silence.[41]

Bernadette had occasionally encountered moments of inner silence, she tells us. They had come and, as fear rose up, gone. But that day those old fears just didn't bubble up and the silence simply remained. She waited, she thought, she stood up, and still the stillness persisted. She walked out of the chapel, "like a feather floats in the wind," and drove home, still in stillness. She's remained in that silence ever since.

For weeks she tried to get a fix on this strange new state of affairs. She asked her teachers, read St. John of the Cross, went to the library. Nothing helped.[42] (Imagine if she'd tried a decade of graduate school!) But coming home from the library,

> *walking downhill with a panorama of valley and hills before me, I turned my gaze inward, and what I saw stopped me in my tracks. Instead of the usual unlocalized center of myself, there was nothing there; it was empty; and at the moment of seeing this there was a flood of quiet joy and I knew, finally I knew what was missing – it was my "self."*[43]

Her old, vague and "unlocalized" center, her sense of a discrete self, that unconscious but comforting sense we all have that we are a thing, a person with a name, an I — *that* had disappeared.

I actually laughed out loud when I read this! I'm not sure if it was her astonishment, her confusion, or her honesty, but her response seemed so wonderfully believable. She had no idea what to make of it. She had no categories to make sense of this newness at the core of who she was, this silence. And her doubt, astonishment and discomfort all seemed so wonderfully human. But finally her discovery that what had shifted was her sense of self, the loss of that unlocalized center, was painfully familiar.

"Yippee," I felt, "I am not alone! There's a league of the transformationally confused!"

One more aspect of her experience was the clincher. At several points she described that she felt like she was wearing something like "3-D glasses."[44] In all my readings, by then in pretty much every major tradition and many minor ones, I'd never seen anyone mention of that odd 3-D sense that I'd first encountered in those clouds over the Mediterranean (p. 48 above). Maybe this aspect of the transformation wasn't just my own private weirdness but somewhat more common and that whatever had happened to me wasn't so damned idiosyncratic after all!

I found a last passage reassuring in another sense. Over the next few years, still with silence inside, she too had to wrestle with some pretty nasty emotional upheavals. On a walk in the mountains, for example,

> *I was aware that all life around me had come to a complete standstill. Everywhere I looked, instead of life, I saw a hideous nothingness invading and strangling the life out of every object and vista in sight. It was a world being choked to death by an insidious void, whereby every remaining movement was but the final throe of death. The sudden withdrawal of life, left in its wake a scene of death, dying and decay [that was] monstrous and terrible to look upon.*[45] *[It was like the world was being overwhelmed by] "icy fingers of an unknown terror and dread"*[46]

I personally have never faced this particular terror. Nonetheless I found this passage powerfully reassuring not for the particulars but for the fact that she too had nearly overwhelming and challenging emotions. I had felt so much initial confusion, I think, because I was both settled inside and still depressed, angry, anxious and afraid sometimes. To hear that she was enmeshed in a great silence yet also churning left me feeling less crazy. Silence isn't necessarily cheery and it may not be "such a joy, such a joy." One can live in a "supreme state" yet have a complex set of perceptions, confusions and emotions.

Thank God: someone else struggles!

Enlightenment: A Definition

There was no eureka moment, no single magic sentence. It was more like coming to hold a mountain aloft by a thousand sticks. In text after classical text, from East and West, in classics from Buddhists, Hindus, Christians and agnostics, from writers ancient and modern, it eventually became obvious.

"Enlightenment," *mokṣa,* Eckhart's *geburt* (the birth of the son in the soul), *nirvana,* the "no self"— are all lionized in glorious and poetic prose. *Mokṣa* is "perfection," it is "absolute." It is "eternal joy," "the immovable," "the end of all suffering" and "such a joy, joy, joy." For the Christians it is to witness something of God is born in the soul. But once I had dug my way through the "glorious gloriousnesses" and the "resplendent resplendents," enlightenment became not some perfect life, but rather a much more specific psycho-physiological transformation.

Enlightenment, as I was seeing it described in countless texts from every major tradition, is *a shift in the relationship between consciousness and its objects.* Enlightenment is the *unmingling of a commingled reality.*

Before the great unmingling, we know only the structure within which we all begin (at least I *think* we all do). We see objects, think thoughts, feel feelings, etc. and in the midst of it all we may be able to sense some vague or "unlocalized" sense of our selves, as Bernadette Roberts puts it. We all begin with consciousness and its objects co-mingled.

This is how it had always been for me until that January afternoon in the Hotel Karina. I suppose I would have pointed to it somewhere in my chest, but I couldn't have picked out consciousness itself. Who or what I was was part of the jumble of experience, and in itself largely inaccessible.

Oh, in peak meditation experiences or in odd moments just before I'd fall asleep, perhaps, I could sense myself as nothing other than consciousness. But these were at best fleeting.

Hinduism calls such short lived moments "*samādhi.*" Yogacara Buddhist texts speak of them as *nirodha samapatti,* the "cessation of perception and feeling." Sufism calls them '*fana*, "the annihilation of thoughts." Meister Eckhart uses the biblical term *gezucket*, rapture, or being without sensory content.[47] In far too many academic books and articles I've called such moments "pure consciousness events."[48]

In these brief moments, one is aware of no particular content for awareness, yet still remains awake inside. Not thinking of anything, aware of no feelings or perceptions, consciousness is left, very simply, alone. And because one is aware of no objects, we might describe the "structure" of experience at those moments as consciousness having *no* relationship between itself and its objects: consciousness alone, no content.

But the second structure is both more complex and more interesting. For this is the first *permanent* shift, the first stage of enlightenment. (There are others to follow, by the way.) Consciousness now perceives itself in itself, and as as *distinct from* and *witness to* everything one sees and does.

To Buddhism this is *Nirvana*, the "blowing out" of the separate self. For Eckhart it is the g*eburt,* the birth of the son in the soul. For Hinduism and Jainism it's *mokṣa,* release. Maharishi used the phrase "cosmic consciousness," a term of painfully embarrassing hubris. For Ramana Maharshi it's the more modest *sahaja* s*amadhi,* "all time *samadhi*."

In it there are two birds, separate and different in kind. One now knows oneself to be spacious, bottomless, open and empty of content. And this new vastness is sensed as separate from everything one sees or thinks. This expanded consciousness is that "for which" there are thoughts and objects. The knower is now steady, waveless, unchanging, and the silent witness to the full parade of life.

The mystic, for that is what one has now become, may not understand the great unmingling, even for many years. Bernadette didn't. I didn't. But a shift of this depth cannot be missed. It is that different.

Life doesn't become perfect though. The great unmingling does not grant one eternal joy (except, perhaps, in a very narrow sense). Life as a whole does not become endless bliss. One's marriage doesn't become perfect. And it doesn't cure baldness.

Expecting such a pot of gold was my mistake, and the mistake of many I suspect. A change in the structure of consciousness, no doubt has, in the long run, implications for how one feels, talks and acts. It may come to involve letting go of that which holds us psychologically, greater happiness or a new attitude towards one's ego, which is how many spiritual modern self-help teachers tend to present it. But such psychological changes were not what I was seeing again and again in the classical texts or in my life. There is a difference between an insight that breaks through and a break through into a different experiential structure. The shift I was seeing in the classics was one of experiential or existential structure.

This a structural shift—modest, understated and peculiar—in what or who we are at heart, a shift in the fundamental way we encounter ourselves and the world is hardly the stuff of inspiring mythology. But it is an unexpected gift of grace. And not at all nothing. Held aright, such a gift makes possible a life well beyond anything we can beforehand imagine.

Confirmation

The last jigsaw piece slipped into place in the early 90s. I'm not sure if I want to tell you this in order to reassure myself, to create more confidence for what I have to say, or because I've promised to tell you the truth and this just happens to be a piece of the story.

About a decade after I had read all those accounts in graduate school, I was invited to several small gatherings of spiritual teachers at the fabulously wealthy Fetzer Institute, which was looking to develop its spiritual programs. I often found myself sitting next to Ram Dass, several years before his stroke. I came to admire him a lot during those weekends. Despite the beads and robes, he was about as humble and as reflective about his own craziness as anyone I've ever met. We were two monkish and neurotic Hin-Jew spiritual teachers, talking about spirituality in a ridiculously sumptuous setting, and we laughed a lot.

During a break I took him aside. I had never been able to talk to anybody about my experiences, I told him, and I wondered him if we could chat.

We sat, knee to knee, in front of a great bay window. I told him about what had begun two decades earlier. I told him about the planes of silence moving down my body. I described the pins and needles in my neck and the tubes unzipping into emptiness. I told him about the changes in my sleep and my vision. I narrated the expansion of silence and of several other shifts I'll tell you about later. And I told him that since I'd left the TM world, I had never had anyone I could turn to for confirmation. He understood. He asked me about the pins and needles and about my meditations.

Finally he said, "Yes, this sounds like what we talk about."

"This is what?"

And looking deep into my eyes with his bottomless gaze and a kindly smile of recognition, he said simply, "yeah, this is that."

One simple sentence, "Yeah, this is that." And all my self-doubts, all my wonderings and confusions and disillusionments simply vanished. "Yeah," he said again, "this is that."

I smiled and thanked him. Then I locked myself in a nearby bathroom and I wept. I just cried and cried. Finally I could stop asking the damn question! I didn't have to wonder if I was imagining things. Finally I could be sure I wasn't making all this up. "Yeah, this is that." What a simple act of love his was.

Nothing inside changed that day. The silence was still silent, the expanse still expanded. But everything changed. Now when I thought about my life or about the silence that had by then grown well beyond my skull, I could now in good conscience compare it to what I was reading or hearing. When I talked with others or encountered new spiritual texts, I could now plausibly use my own experience as a touchstone. (Indeed I could now begin this book with a bit more confidence.) And I could stop the endless tumblings of self-doubt.

There was probably also a little ego in my weeping as well. I have to admit I liked (and still like) being able to think of myself in that heady light.

Sometimes I'm sorry that I didn't buttonhole Maharishi back in the day and ask him if the shift of that January *was* the much ballyhooed "cosmic consciousness." It sure would have saved me many years of wondering.

But no, on second thought I'm not sorry. Painful though it was, all my confusion and self-doubt led me into graduate school, into the philosophy of mysticism and into the academic debates in which I played some role, the so called Katz-Forman debates (see below). I did it all in part to resolve my life-perplexities. Had Maharishi looked at me and smiled, "Yes, dis is dat," I would no doubt have stopped wondering. But then I wouldn't have had the privilege of asking my questions, my way.

I became pretty cynical in that first decade after the great unmingling. When I was a young graduate student, I "knew" that enlightenment talk was just self-talk, just a way to gussy up hope.

But like the Buddha outside my window, emptiness has a way of persisting. It simply remained all those years, half-forgotten, patient, present. I dismissed it and I got all cynical about it and I reduced it to neuro-physiological quirks so that I would sound all smart and knowledgeable. It just waited, in the background, steady, constant, unobtrusive. And pulling ever so slightly. It drew me slowly out of my clever cynicism and out of my disillusionments.

It just remained as what it was, growing imperceptibly year by year, witnessing it all, whispering its quiet music into my life.

I was in real trouble in my twenties: desperate, half suicidal, anxious without letup. No wonder silence was not enough. It did not provide good mothering and it did not lead to happiness. It did not make my marriage work, my stocks go up, or my anxieties fade away. For anyone in real pain, I doubt it would have been enough.

Because it wasn't what I had hoped for, I missed what it was. Breaking out of the endless layers of a chattering mind, untangling the self from its content, even in just a tiny sliver, was, I now realize, a gift of enormous value.

For permanent silence offers real access to That which is not us. Contact with the really real, perhaps even with God, is a rare privilege. It is warmth and strength and peace in a storm-tossed mind and a fragile world.

Over the nearly four decades it has now been at my core, I have come to rely on its presence. I count on its steadiness, lean on its good humored simplicity, occasionally enjoy its visual depth. But because I was looking for a cure for heartaches, I missed what it was.

So yeah, Ram Dass, this is it. This is the open consciousness. This is that which is other and divine. This is the infinite planted within as consciousness itself. And I just didn't know. It was too ambiguous, too paradoxical. But its very ordinariness makes it that much more real.

I doubt there is a one size fits all here. I suspect that the great unmingling can come as a whole orchestra, when the stars and suns swirl into a unity with the soul. Some seem to become suddenly wise or clever or charismatic. Others of us, not so much. But the great unmingling, the separation of witness from object so final it remains even through the deepest sleep, is, I think, the same for everyone, no matter what the religion.

It would take many years for it to soak thoroughly into my body, years more to weave it into the rest of my life. That process is not yet complete; I doubt it will ever be. But the vastness that so transformed my life, seated comfortably on my couch in the Hotel Karina, is the same as I sense sitting here this evening in front of the dimming embers and warmth. And probably the same everywhere.

It was just a tiny opening, the merest kiss. But it was a kiss of the real.

And even a tiny candle-flame begins to light the darkness.

Part II.
Quo Vadis

The Question

So there I was, four years into graduate school, a decade after the great unmingling, having studied all these traditional accounts of mokṣa, Nirvana and Christ Consciousness, now confident I knew what the word "enlightenment" actually pointed to. And now facing one enormous question. Well three actually.

The first question was this: when you get the pot of gold that you wanted and it's not what you thought, well, what then *is* it?

Whatever had happened to me, and now I was pretty sure this was at least a good chunk of the enlightenment for which I had been longing so avidly, it was not enough. It didn't make me chipper. It didn't end my troubles. It didn't make me good at my job. It didn't even make it clear which job I should be doing. Even carrying an infinite silence, I wasn't better off in any obvious way than any other broke graduate student. Paul McCartney's "such a joy, joy, joy" this wasn't! No wonder I didn't dance for joy back when it began.

Yet, I also knew even then, nor was it nothing. Something did seem to be happening inside. A quiescence — permanent, kindly and slowly expanding—at the level of your own awareness is...well... new. I was a different kind of being than I had been, though I couldn't say quite how. I couldn't understand much of it, but nor could I deny it. In my everyday life, it wasn't at all obvious what practical difference this strange new way of living really meant. So here was my first question: What real difference does this sort of shift make?

The post modern version of this same question is this: as described by the Upanishads, the Buddhist texts, Daoism and other spiritual teachers, millions of human beings have shaped their lives around the search for the enlightenment. Have all those people merely assured themselves that there is enlightenment and then striven to answer the question that they themselves had posed? Is there any there there?

My second question grew out of the first. If this ain't "it," then what is? If "enlightenment" as the East describes it or the "heaven on earth" that the West describes just aren't, for us, complete spiritual goals, then what might be? For folks like me, who live a post modern, post Freudian, post true-believer, sexually active, mortgaged life, what might be *a* or perhaps *the* plausible spiritual goal? What is a *telos* worth pursuing? What are or should we complex westerners really be after today?

And my third question: how do we get *that?* If daily meditation or Yoga or Tai Chi aren't enough to get us to that more plausible spiritual goal, what practice or set of practices might?

As I'm sitting here, warm in my hermitage, it occurs to me that my questions were not unconnected to the fact that I'm here in Western New York, and here in the 21st Century. I'm an American, a westerner. I'm neither Hindu, Buddhist nor Daoist. And I don't live in a monastery (though this is pretty close!). Enlightenment was an answer to a problem that traditional Hindus and Buddhists had: the resolution of *samsara*. They assumed that we all live and die and then get ourselves reborn again. And then we live, die again and get reborn again. And again. … without end. Their question was, how do we get off the mouse wheel?

The answer for a Hindu or Buddhist was enlightenment. If you metaphysically *separate* yourself from that which suffers, if you stop identifying with the self that gets reborn, you will become free of the endless cycle of rebirth.

Nice answer. But not my question. To me rebirth is an interesting possibility. But on what happens after you die, for me the jury is still out. Maybe we get reborn. Maybe we go to heaven or hell. Or maybe we don't. Certainly how to come to terms with death, bereavement and loss are important matters, for sure! But what happens after you die is not my life-issue.

My issue, and the issue of most western, modern folks I know, has something to do with living. My spiritual questions have to do with how to live a life, if you will, or perhaps how to live with others. How do we be happy or satisfied? How do we live well in our marriages, our friendships, our workdays? How do we find fulfillment? When we heard about "eternal contentment,"[49] what we wanted was an answer to our longings for personal, *individual* satisfaction.

What I was looking for, what we were all looking for, I think, would have to have here and now practical value. I personally wanted to end my depression and resolve my anxieties. I wanted a great relationship. We wanted meaning in a complex urban life and work worth doing. Our questions had to do with finding find real, living, full-bodied fulfillment and lightness in our shoes.

And if enlightenment as I came to understand it wasn't by itself doing this, then what will? And how?

So here are the triple questions that I have been asking and trying to answer with my life.

1. What actual, practical differences do shifts like these make?
2. If such existential shifts aren't enough for us, given who we are and how we think, what might be enough?
3. How do we foster *that*?

These are deep and difficult matters and well worth answering. Not so that we can grade each other or ourselves. (God forbid!) Not so we can gloat. (Even worse!) No, it is important to get a fix on our *telos*, our life-goals, to understand where we are (or should be) headed. In which direction do we point our horse?

Once we know where we want to go, it becomes easier to understand how to get there. And even if we never get to the final *telos* (even if we probably never will) at least we'll be moving in roughly the right direction. *Quo vadis*?

Chapter 4

Learning to Live It

Working in It

I'm looking out over the snowy hills this morning. The sun is peering meekly through the graying cloud layer; it looks like it might snow.

I'm not thinking as I'm writing these words. I'm *feeling* as opposed to *planning* what I need to write. A phrase, "I'm looking out over the snowy hills" comes to mind and with it comes a vaguely directional feeling. That means, I know, that it's time to start jotting down.

Writing here is more like listening than creating. What I feel is a kind of poise. I pause, listening for what seems real to be present. In such a poise I seem to be able to remain connected with the quietness that is nudging me. I think a sentence, but stop—it too clever—then wait again for what is true to waft up. Mostly I find myself in a kind of alert patience, settled, largely without words. So I sit, the clouds grey and the day chilly, my pen in hand, waiting patiently still into this kindness of love.

When I entered graduate school the dominant approach was the post modernism I learned so painfully at the feet of Professor Proudfoot. In the realm of religious experiences, that meant that we encounter what we *expect* to encounter. The main exponent of this doctrine in the study of mysticism was a fellow named Steven Katz, whose *Mysticism and Philosophical Analysis* had just come out.[50] Into everything we see, think or do, his argument ran, we carry our enormous set of assumptions, beliefs, habits and expectations. I simply assume that the liquid in the cup will be warm but not scalding, that the pen in my hand will not break into pieces and that the lady in the cottage down the hill will not suddenly lob a grenade my way. We learned to expect such things are from our cultures, our parents, our experiences and our teachers. We need to, so we don't have to figure out again and again what a teacup or a pen is for or how to use them. When we want to use them we can just pick these things up, barely notice them, and drink our tea or write. I both see and don't see most of my world, really, for I assume a great deal about things. As Coleridge put this, the mind "half sees and half creates."

Like that we learn about Brahman, God or the Tao at the feet of our teachers, rabbis, texts and ceremonies, Katz's theory goes. When we have a mystical experience we will encounter just that which we've learned from our religious or spiritual traditions. A Catholic, for example, hears about Christ, sin and salvation, a Hindu about colorful gods, formless Brahman and worshipful gurus. And bingo bango boggin, when each has a mystical moment, they'll encounter just these "things." Our expectations help create not just the way we talk about our experiences, but very contours and content of our experience itself. A spiritual person's

> *experience itself as well as the form in which it is reported, is shaped by concepts which the mystic brings to, and which shape his experience.*[51]

We actually see Christ or formless Brahman, not just talk about our experience in these terms. Or as Katz's colleague Robert Gimello put this, we build up our expectations and then we psycho-somatically "enhance" them into what we see:

> *[A] mystical experience is simply the psychosomatic enhancement of religious beliefs and values or of beliefs and values of other kinds which are held 'religiously.'*[52]

Our long history and training and expectations prepares the ground for, and probably even shapes the neural pathways, that create our religious experiences.

In my own case, I had been trained to expect such things as inward silence, meditation, a shift into enlightenment, etc. And with a slight of brain-hand, I then encountered just these things.

One day, while I was pondering all this, I was sitting on the grass of Columbia University's quadrangle, watching a robin peck after some tasty morsel. I'm something of a birder and I've watched a zillion Robins, so I knew in a quick glance it was a Robin. They have dusky orange breasts, I knew, straight backed posture, and bob at the ground. I didn't need to look at him very carefully to know he was a robin. In fact he was pretty far away and I was no doubt "filling in" most of what I couldn't actually see. I was indeed "half seeing and half creating" him, I thought, something I do whenever I see something familiar: grass, the student union building, my sneakers.[53]

But, it occurred to me, I'm not so familiar with *every* bird I encounter. Sometimes I've seen new birds: a Yellow Rumped Warbler, say, or a Harlequin Duck. When I see one of these tasty little morsels I have to look at him or her pretty carefully, checking back and forth with my *Birds of North America,* if only to figure out what I'm looking at. I don't fill in nearly as much of a rare Harlequin Duck. I have to attend pretty carefully to his color, markings, beak and quack to distinguish him from other ducks. I don't supply as much from my background expectations.

Then I went on to myself: let's say I see a bird that *no one* has ever seen. Let's say he has the beak of a duck, roars like a lion and flies like a jet. To that speedy little bugger I'd have to pay very, very careful attention. I'd fill in virtually nothing from my past experience, or anyone's for that matter.

There seems to be a continuum here, I thought. To some perceptions I will supply a lot from my side. To others I'll supply less. And when I look at something truly new, I'll supply virtually nothing. The more I supply, the less I actually see. And vice versa.

But what I encountered on that loveseat in the Hotel Karina was utterly *unlike* whatever I had come to expect. Even today it's hard to understand. So whatever it was, it was too queer and unfamiliar to be the kind of thing that I could have cooked up with my psychosomatic enhancements. Similarly for Bernadette Roberts; what she encountered was so off her expectation grid that she could never have pre-formed it. I suspect that the sense of novelty and surprise is almost always part of these transformations. Whatever wrongheaded expectations we come with will create something else. Wrong expectations will do a crummy design job.

So no, I don't cook up every experience, I thought as I watched the Robin fly away. Some experiences I shape a lot, some less, and a few are genuinely unexpected. When we encounter something off our chart, our prior expectations just can't be creating it. We cannot cook up what we cannot imagine.

That insight became the core of the argument that drove me to write or edit four books between 1982 and 1995, some 30 articles, and deliver more than 50 professional talks, not counting endless classrooms.[54] That's about as much excitement as we academics get!

This argument, if you think about it, is basically negative: spiritual experiences are *not* created by our expectations, *not* by our assumptions, *not* by our language. To some extent, this is the only way I could make such a point. For the emptiness itself is not *in* language, not *within* our thought system. What I was doing, I now see, was to make the only space I could for the very wordless emptiness that had planted itself my life.

But I had to. I could do nothing other than to try to make such an argument, now that I think of it. When I read the post modernists, it was just obvious that I hadn't created the silence; *it* had planted itself in my life. I could do nothing else than harness the philosophical tools I was learning to make room for what was obvious to me. Or rather, silence was making room for itself, in some sense *through* me. I was in effect working to allow it to winnow itself forward into my academic world.

"Knowing this, the wise can speak of nothing else," says the

Upanishads. I could do nothing else than try to give the sacred in my life a voice, however flawed and halting. I simply can't imagine having some permanent experience of the vast openness and *not* trying to "speak it" in a way that felt deeply right to me.[55] Every generation has its own context and language, and we all have to speak it out in our way.

This didn't mean I was, from my side, confident. I didn't have much trust in my abilities. I wasn't sure we'd win the day (which I like to think we have in the long run). But I never doubted the real point, that the vastness is the real deal and beyond what we can know or shape.

As a result, speaking and allowing silence to grow into my life has become my life's work. Making philosophical space for it, writing books about it, learning to live and to teach others how to live it in their everyday lives, etc. Indeed it has led to this book. Speaking silence in the soul has become my life's calling.

Finding a life's calling, at least in the way I understand, is more like listening than creating. You listen for that which wants to be spoken through you. You allow it to emerge, listening for what the Hindus call your "*dharma*", your deep and natural calling. If you're lucky, you come to orient your work around what is most deeply true, allowing it to do its work through you.

There is a kind of ease and freedom in doing this. Work takes on a deep soul resonance. Doing work that reverberates the truth allows you to do your days with a kind of depth that I doubt can be there without it. The sense here is of being a kind of tube, the energy from what is deepest coursing up through your torso. It's like all your cells are aligned, down to your core. Because there's no interior struggle about it, no deep doubts, working with coherence around what is most deeply true brings a sense of ease and freedom with it.

Of course, I've worked my tail off. Lots of long days, endless editing, years and years of organizing and teaching. To rise to a calling requires effort as well as listening. But working with nearly cellular alignment with what is at my core, has had, I think, a resonance and an ease beyond what I could have otherwise known.

I couldn't have said any of this back then. I was too busy learning the material and making the arguments. But here, perhaps, was the first hint of an answer to my question, of what use, really, is silence? For what was driving me to do this work, I feel just now, what became the general direction of my thoughts, wasn't *me*. It was the silence itself. I don't know how, exactly, but it was nudging me all along. "Say it," it whispered. "Say it in a way that expresses what is so. Don't be satisfied with someone else's version of what is so. Don't stop at a partial answer. Speak it so that you can stand in effortless and full-bodied alignment with what is deepest. Say it as well as you can in a way that others can understand. But say it."

If silence is to part of our everyday lives, we have to somehow learn to work from within it. Our work is too important, our workdays too many, to do anything else. There is a calling for each of us, I think, to speak what is deepest, in our way. It nudges and pushes and calls until we answer. And then it nudges some more.

Coming up to the Line

Sometime in the middle of developing my philosophical arguments, roughly eight years after the bottomlessness had established itself as a sliver in the back of my neck, it had grown. It *thickened*, as I've mentioned, to now fill the back half of my head. By about 5 years more, well into graduate school, it had come to fill up my whole skull, as if that wormhole to infinity now filled my cranium, from eyes to the nape of my neck.

This slow growth of silence was more physical than anything else. It became more tactile—a velvety, cottony translucence. It was not an emotional shift though. I still got dangerously anxious, for example, while dealing with some imperious professor. Yvonne and I still collided over one triviality after another. I still fretted endlessly over money, always a problem in the graduate student's life, still fantasized about women, still got impatient at cash registers. Whatever this slowly expanding openness might have been, it sure wasn't that personality transplant I'd wanted.

Yet it did seem to be having effects on more than my head or my philosophizing. I could focus on my reading a little longer. Perhaps this was because I was actually interested in the history of Buddhism or in answering post modern philosophy. But the quieting of internal chatter couldn't but help.

It seemed to be getting easier to sit down to study, and to write my seminar papers. I wasn't quite so panicky when I looked for part time teaching jobs. And when I finally landed my first teaching job at The New School, my teaching was surprisingly easy and, I believe, effective.

Things were improving, in part no doubt, because I was developing professional skills and slowly becoming more of a contributing member of society. I was starting to give papers at professional conferences, starting to get articles published, was writing two books and was by now raising two kids. The confidence I was feeling was no doubt in part because I was now actually doing life. But I can't help believing that the slowly expanding silence was helping.

Then one day, as I was walking across 114th street towards Columbia University, I suddenly realized that I was not anxious.

I hadn't just received an A on a paper. Some cute girl hadn't just flirted with me. Nothing had changed at home. Yet just for a few seconds, with no obvious cause, I felt, to some real surprise, *neutral.*

For most people, I suppose, a few moments without anxiety is nothing special. But to me that moment was astonishing! I still find it hard to believe, but up until that instant, ever since I'd been a kid, I had felt the pull of that mewling sinking feeling every waking moment of every day!

Anxiety at this level, with you no matter what you are doing, sucks the air out of your lungs, pulls at your thighs, shrivels your heart. I was worried in the 7th grade whether Stewart C. liked me. I'd freeze utterly in the 9th grade, unable to dial that last digit of Peggy K's phone number. I was terribly anxious in college, worried constantly about the next class, the next grade, or whether I would ever get off my orange naugahide chair. I was anxious about love, anxious I was too fat, worried about money, afraid that I'd miss the subway. Anxiety like this, steady, generalized and pointless, hovers around like a pathetic beggar, stealing your life.

But there I was, for just a few astonished seconds, without any anxiety. It's amazing to say this now, but honestly, I didn't know it was possible.

"Hey," I said to myself, "I'm not anxious!" And of course, I immediately got anxious that I'd get anxious again. And so I was.

Perhaps two or three years later, it occurred to me that, "you know, I don't think I've been anxious all morning." Again, no new job, no article accepted, no stock market killing. Just a whole morning, untroubled. And, I sensed, it hadn't been the first.

Around the end of my graduate career, 1988, it was, "you know, I don't seem to get anxious much these days." It was slow. But it was real.[56]

By no means were all my troubles resolved. Papers, worries what I'd do after graduation, Dr. Proudfoot's respect, marriage tensions, parenting issues—all were, alas, still very much with me. It was more that the background tone of my life was softening. Not that I was actually happy, mind you. Just no longer always afraid.

Here again was a hint of value in what had befallen me years before. It was as if that unflickering candle-flame beneath my life, imperceptible though it was, was helping to slowly melt the ice within which I had been frozen. Just the tiniest warmth. But even a Candleflame, if steady enough long enough, can melt an iceberg.

Chapter 5

Feeling

It and Ducks

Coming up the icy drive last night, my car slid helplessly back down the hill towards the pond and ended up perched over a ditch. I'm waiting for the tow truck to come, feeling at once a little foolish and like laughing. If I tell the real truth, I'm somewhat ashamed too: What's wrong with me that I couldn't get my car up the hill? Why did I let my tires get so bald? I'm feeling very much the incompetent kid, waiting for daddy to come in his big tow truck and make it all better! And like giggling.

It's a kind of dance I'm in just now. With the frigid window on one side and the warm stove on the other, the heat and the cold and the embarrassment and the silence and the giggles and the shame are all jumbled together at once. No one feeling dominates. There is a kind of flowing ease between them all, embarrassment becoming chill becoming silence becoming …

The ease I feel in flowing from sensations to thoughts to silence to feelings seems of a piece with the ease that dawned all those years ago in Mallorca. I don't have to *try* to be open in the silence. I just am. And I am not working here to make these feelings and impressions flow. I am nearly as effortless in the face of all these sensations and emotions as I am to It.

It didn't used to be like this. Despite finding a dharma, a calling, I was struggling in my thirties to avoid experiencing some pretty nasty, out-of-control feelings. The most pressing of these came up around class work. Oh, my grades were fine, actually, but every time I'd turn in a paper, see a professor in the hall or open a test booklet, my heart would race.

I remember standing in front of Professor Proudfoot's office one day, for example, actually shaking. "He'll trash the paper" I'd just handed him, I thought. "He'll rip apart the section on Russell." "He'll tell me I didn't understand metaphysics" (something that was true). "He'll trash some sloppy footnotes." "He just won't like it!" and I'd wonder what on earth I had been thinking when I turned it in and or why the hell I had come to graduate school in the first place? He'd kick me out of Columbia for sure this time, and I'd be ashamed and end up broke and homeless and ...

And I had no idea how to get off the obsessional mouse wheel.

My fear of professors grew and grew over the first years of graduate school. I should find a psychotherapist, I kept thinking.

But meditation would take care of it, I kept telling myself. Meditation relieves stress. And I carry the silence. It'll be fine.

But the day I stood in front of Professor Proudfoot's office actually shaking in a full blown panic attack was something new. It was time.

I don't know about other people, but for me deciding to go to a psychotherapist as an adult was an huge deal. Going now meant that I wasn't OK, that meditation hadn't done it all, that silence didn't fix everything. Despite a decade and a half of regular meditation and a decade of inward spaciousness, it meant I was in trouble.

I had come to the end of a dream, standing at that door: the comforting fiction that it'll all be better, or the solace that silence is enough. It was another disillusionment, but one notch deeper.

Yet standing at that doorway was its own kind of beginning as well, I can see from here. With that declaration, that it was time, I took the first step on my own path. I was now beginning to *apply* what I'd discovered with the vastness in my own way. I was answering the whisper I think we all feel, to live it everywhere, to find a way to flow, wherever we are blocked. And that moment was when I began to answer it in my way.

There are no more systems, no more masters at this point. You just sense the whisper "you are blocked here too," and try whatever you can to find your way. "Keep going," is all it says, "even though your beliefs say you aren't supposed to need to. Keep going, for you are still resisting, still in pain, still hurting others. Keep going."

It wasn't long before I was standing in front of another door, this one to the comfortingly rumpled West Side office of Dr. Ken Ruge, a highly recommended psychotherapist. It was from Ken that I learned the term "panic attack," and it took months of weekly sessions to get a handle on them.

What I discovered there, of course, had to do with my past, my particular family and my own confusions. Be it enough to say that there had been enormous stress in my family on competence and success, I discovered, and I was afraid of being neither. My father the businessman used to say that the "only way you can keep score in life is the size of the bank account." When he would talk about someone whose didn't have as high a "score" as he—an MSW, a psychotherapist, an artist or teacher—he would refer to them with a wave of his hand and a little puff of air, as if he was brushing away a dust ball. His key to success was to take control and to, as he put it, "keep all your ducks in a row."

To stand in front of Professor Proudfoot's door was to be written off behind that hand wave. I wasn't running from graduate school or some lanky professor. I was running from Dad's disapproval, from disappearing. It was the unfilled longings from childhood I was panicky about, that that I'd never be seen, never exist.

Our spiritual traditions, and silence itself, may cure the confusion between consciousness and its contents. But it doesn't cure old self images, doesn't make us feel worthy when we never have, doesn't put our footnotes in order. And it certainly cannot provide the respect of someone you admire.

John Welwood catches the mistake best:

> *While spiritual traditions generally explain the cause of suffering in general terms as the result of ignorance, faulty perception, or disconnection from our true nature, Western psychology provides a more specific developmental understanding. It shows how*

suffering stems from childhood conditioning, in particular, from static and distorted images of self and other that we carry with us in the baggage of our past.

No, the solution here couldn't come from meditation or prayer or Yoga poses. I had to feel how afraid I was of those ducks getting out of their rows and feel that desperate longing for approval. I had to feel that hand wave, dread it, feel it wipe me out of existence. And then feel it some more.

Only after I had named my fear and felt that puff of air, only when I had laughed at those ducks, did I eventually find myself sitting in front of Professor Proudfoot's door, having turned in a paper on Buddhist Epistemology, just waiting. No constricted throat, I noticed, no rapid heartbeat. Oh, I still fully expected him to rip my paper apart. A good professor, which he was, does that. But, I saw with astonishment, I was just seated there, calm, patient, erect.

Sitting in front of that door, erect in my chair, it occurred to me, was just like the silence itself. I was simple at that moment, patient, just there, like the inward steadiness. It took no effort to wait like that, as it takes no effort to live the silence.

Nothing flashy. No neon lights or crashing symbols. Just where there had been fear and churning, there was now simplicity.

"That's interesting," I said to myself with a smile.

It and Sexuality

After I had pretty much resolved the panic attacks, I kept on with therapy. I knew even larger issues loomed, mostly having to do with my terribly confused relationships with the female of the species. Maybe all men struggle here, and all women in their way, I don't know. But I sure did.

Even though I'd been married nearly a decade, I was anything but easy around the woman I lived with. And I still found myself often lost in some pretty intense daydreams — women I knew, women I saw on the subway, women I'd dated long ago — angry, horny, needy, even, I am embarrassed to admit, rape fantasies. Sometimes I'd come out breathing hard, terrified of my own violence. Clearly silence wasn't curing the boy/girl matter.

Nor did silence cure the sexual perturbations of the guru gang either, I knew even then. Tibetan Lama Chogyam Trungpa Rinpoche, for example, who was reported to got so drunk sometimes that he had to be helped off the stage, was said to have slept openly with female disciples. His "dharma heir," Osel Tendzin, not only had frequent sex with his students, but also supposedly hid from them that he had the AIDS virus and could infect them. The abbot of the San Francisco Zen Center, Richard Baker Roshi, lost his job over his repeated affairs with female disciples, including, I heard, his best friend's wife. The founder of the Hindu Siddha Yoga movement, Swami Muktananda, reportedly slept with some of his pre-pubescent disciples.

Out of 54 Buddhist, Hindu and Jain teachers in the United States, according to psychologist Jack Kornfield, only 15 had lived up to their tradition's proscriptions of celibacy.[57] Of the sexually active 39, some 34 had affairs with current students.

Five of the six most esteemed Zen Buddhist masters in the United States, who presumably were selected by an enlightened teacher abroad to teach, were involved in grossly self-centered and conspicuously unenlightened behavior."[58]

Then there were the western ministers. They don't talk about enlightenment much, but they do emphasize chastity, the sanctity of marriage and their own faith. But Evangelical preacher Jimmy Swaggart railed on and on about sex, loss of "family values" and prostitution, while surreptitiously frequenting prostitutes. Colorado Evangelist Ted Haggard preached vociferously against the "vile sin of homosexuality" while himself engaging in a three year relationship with a gay prostitute. New age Rabbi Mordechai Gafni was seductive enough to cause him to resign his position in Israel's Bayit Chadash in disgrace.[59] And strangest of all, an Iranian mullah, Hojatoleslam Hasan Golestani, taped himself having sex with his friend's wife![60]

And we cannot forget the 4,392 men, some 4% of American Catholic priests, who were accused of being pedophiles.[61]

What's going on here?

It is too easy to answer that all these sexual misadventures are just the fault of a few bad apples.

That would be true. But the failure here is deeper, and it's time to say so.

Spiritual enlightenment, religious transformation, being twice born just may be, with reference to sexual issues, incomplete.

Enlightenment or being saved by God is important. It is the great unmingling, a revelation of our connection with the divine or some underlying energy: Brahman, Buddha-mind, Tao, God, the ultimate. I believe this was what our traditions were celebrating. And it was, apparently enough for most of history. But in our highly sexualized, post pill, post feminine liberation, it is no longer enough.

After all, gurus, rabbis and ministers in 1150 or 1850 or even 1950 didn't face what we must on a daily basis. They had to confront their own sexual urges, for sure. But, occasional stories like David and Bathsheba notwithstanding, opportunities for sexual relationships were relatively limited. The sexual urges of monks and nuns were encountered largely in the privacy of their own cells and single-gendered monasteries. Although the sexuality of the religious was probably always *an* issue, for most of history one's personal issues with sexuality probably wasn't *the* dominant life-issue.

> *In the traditional cultures of Asia, it was a viable option for a yogi to pursue spiritual development apart from worldly involvement, or to live purely as the impersonal universal, without having much of a personal life or transforming the structures of that life. These older cultures provided a religious context that honored and supported spiritual retreat and placed little or no emphasis on individual concerns.*

Their life's challenge had to do with something broader, about sin more broadly or ignorance and on a metaphysical salvation. Most traditions, especially Eastern religions, focused especially on universal love and transcending the personal. Which could, in my experience, easily lead to a kind of avoidance.[62]

But few of us are monks any more or cloistered, and today, with miniskirts and washboard abs, sexuality is constantly stressed. We simply cannot avoid the issue of sexuality, and in our post-Freud era, deny our conscious and unconscious drives. If indeed we ever could, we can no longer transcend the personal.[63]

Frankly I think that the spiritual challenge of today is greater than it was in traditional times. We have to confront our own and other people's sexuality every day, overtly and often publically, on the streets, on the TV, in the theatres and on the internet.

And sex, though more readily available today, is, especially for spiritual teachers, far more dangerous. In ancient times when a spiritual leader committed a sexual or some other peccadillo, their disciples would be likely to try to keep it under wraps, either because that was the tradition, or because they believed it to have a deeper spiritual logic (as in, "he did it to raise our spiritual consciousness or through the wonderfully slippery "Crazy Wisdom" excuse) or to protect their masters' reputation, or all of the above.[64]

But today we are less cowed by authority.[65] In our era of the suspicion of power, gotcha journalism and (one hopes) greater sensitivity to sexual harassment, wayward priests or roshis are more likely to be outted, humiliated and even arrested. Sexual peccadilloes today are dangerous for your neighborhood guru.

I like to believe that most of our spiritual teachers and ministers have indeed undergone deep inner shifts. But if so, it's obvious that such shifts do not lead to transparent and healthy enough sexual lives. Enlightenment or being twice born is, as I said, no longer enough.

The complete life, the good human life, must, I'm coming to see, include both a transformed inner life *and* a transformed outer life. To be complete our spiritual goal must include both a deep inner freedom *and* enough self-awareness to recognize when we're feeling or acting in ways that are stuck or corrupt. And it must include the courage to actually change.

Spirit and psyche address different aspects of the complete life: the unconditioned and inward is not the same as the personal and conditioned.

> *Spiritual practice, especially mysticism, points toward a timeless trans-human reality, while psychological work addresses the evolving human realm, with all its issues of personal meaning and interpersonal relationship.*[66]

If we are to live a full, sane, complete life, we will have to heal both today.

OK, lets talk about sex. I want to say at the outset that I am not completely clean about sexuality, by which I mean being both open and alive to it yet with clear and impeccable boundaries. Since the real issues around sexuality are quite taboo in our society, it is hard to say, but it's my impression that *very* few of us live a fully clean, healthy sexuality.

All I can claim is that I am a lot cleaner than I used to be. And I am because of a long process that began about six months after resolving my panic about professors. I was in Ken's office when I noticed a curtain rod and dark curtain hanging in a window across the street. "Funny," I remarked to him almost in passing, "it looks like belts."

That billowing curtain caught my eye again a couple of weeks later. It reminded me even more clearly of the belt rack in my closet when I was a kid, and I suddenly felt terrified. I flashed on my mother towering over me.

"What's this about?" I wondered aloud to Ken. "I keep seeing this image of my mother standing over me, with a belt raised over her head. What on earth? …"

Over the next few weeks, in and out of sessions, I found myself preoccupied with that billowing curtain and belts. Images of my preteen bedroom came in and out of focus: black and white checkered bedspread, dark mahogany desk, white muslin curtains. And flashes of my mother, towering above like the terrifying Hindu goddess Kali, raising a belt.

Slowly, in bits and pieces, and with enormous waves of belly-sinking dread, I began to bring to mind what I was forbidden to remember. I'm maybe 10 or 12 and hadn't picked up my clothes, or had come to dinner ten minutes late, or had brought home some teacher's note saying I'd joked around in class. And my mother would come flying into my bedroom in a rage.

"What is this, a pig sty?"

"Why did you embarrass me in front of my friends?" she'd yell, damn near beet red.

"You won't amount to anything!"

"What's *wrong* with you?"

And then there was *the* night. She'd found the leather suitcase in which I'd stashed the pile of "girly magazines" some 7th grade friend had laid on me. She careened nearly apoplectic into my room, climbed onto my chair, thrown it down from the top shelf and began heaving the magazines around the room.

"How could you even look at such filth?" she raged, throwing glossy bits of breast and torso across the floor like feces.

"I don't know," I said weakly, "Jack gave them to me."

"What are you some kind of pervert?" she raged. And by now in full histrionic, she chanted:

"You want to see naked women? .... I'll *show* you a naked woman!" and with that began to pull her nightgown over her head …

"No Mom, stop!"

She relented, probably ashamed at her own jealous fury ... then she reached over to the belt rack in my closet, grabbed the widest belt and raised it over her head …

I hid under my pillow… afraid, disgusted, embarrassed, shivering from the terrifying intensity and betrayal …

I turned and looked up, and watched that belt snaking high above her head, time nearly frozen. I heard it whine through the air and felt it sharp and hot on my back. I heard her grunt again with effort and felt more than heard it creasing through the air a second time, and a third ...

In the safety of Ken's love, I relived those moments again and again. I heard the yelling. I felt the heat on my back… I smelled the pillow, felt the leather. I even shivered again. I told him every gory detail I could dredge up. I told Yvonne. I scribbled new details into my journal. I felt it again, told it again. I felt the queer let down that is betrayal. I felt the chest heat of the anger I had not been allowed to admit. I felt the fear. I felt the loneliness.

I came to see how and why I had to push it all out of my memory. To tell anyone, even to remember it, would have been too dangerous to her, to the family, to me. No wonder I had such violent day dreams! And could this be what those whispering voices had been trying to tell me, two decades before?

The first friend I told was Phil Goldberg. I got so choked up I could hardly get through the story. When I shared it with Glenn and

Peggy a year later, I could tell it just a notch easier.

By four years later the heat had pretty much seeped out of the balloon. I came to be able to tell the story reasonably straight, feel the whacking or remember those magazines without reacting all that much.

By now it's just part of my history; it's almost emotionally neutral. I still tell the tale every now and again. But now I use it to make a point, as I'm doing here. I own *it* now, not the other way round.

Though painful as hell, to remember such confusing childhood events or even traumas in enough detail to drain them of their sepsis is an enormous gift. It is an essential step in coming to terms with those very ancient, very human, drives. I can't see who they can get cleaned up without being faced.

I may be wrong, but I doubt a Shankara or a St. Theresa or a Muslim mystic like Rabi'a ever knew to confront such personal issues.[67] Before Freud we human beings just didn't know about the long-lasting effects of our fathers being distant or our mothers overly solicitous, or that we had to be overachievers to be loved. Nor did we know, as a species, that our childhood horrors lose their power over us only when we bring them, in all their gory detail, to full conscious light.

There's no fault in this. Humanity just didn't know. Our great teachers lived before words like "ego" or "superego" came to mean quite what they do today.[68]

Without the frame of psycho-therapy, without knowing how their individual concerns and history shaped or scarred them, no wonder our ancient spiritual teachers thought that gaining an impersonal Brahman or the Divine was enough.

But it is no longer enough. We must invite in our individual histories, especially where they were painful, and untangle our personal confusions in order to become free, effortless human beings. We know this now. The deepest spiritual awareness or the encounter with the divine do not by themselves salve our personal wounds, resolve our sexual conundrums or cure our inappropriate behaviors.

Silence alone, Christ Consciousness alone, addresses none of this. The checks on my childhood bedspread, the color of my mothers' fingernails, the welts I could not allow myself to remember but could not forget—none were to be found in the empty bottomlessness. Silence and shadows, grace and grit, dwell in different domains of reality.

It was only in bringing the pain of those forbidden memories to the light of consciousness that I began the long process of welcoming and becoming larger than them. Only when I saw and said and wept it all out again and again did the toxicity of all those events begin to melt and my sexuality begin to be just another part of who I am. Only then could I begin the lifelong task of learning to integrate my wonderful sex drive into who I am while being free of its hold.

What strikes me today as I sit, still waiting for that tow truck in this riot of memories and chill and silence and even some subtle horny feelings, is how non-resistant I feel to them all. Nothing is in the way; these urges, feelings and memories just flow and flow. There's much I cannot allow myself to feel, not that I can sense anyway. I doubt I could have welcomed all these urges and feelings quite as easily had I not confronted my own fear and shame and pain back then, and brought it out of my own hidings. And this non-resistance, this easiness with my once-secret pain, is precisely the same non-resistance that is part of the silence itself.

If we are to become free I don't know any other way than to free ourselves from the grip of what is for us unspeakable, loosen the chains of our own desperation. And learn to laugh with it all.

Living thus effortlessly is what the Taoists call *wu wei,* effortless action. To be complete, such effortlessness must be wide armed enough to welcome all of our personalities, drives and scarred histories. It demands willingness, standing in the fire long enough to speak every last bit of truth, until its toxicity is pretty much burnt off. Only then will we be free in the face of our own forbidden emotions.

It's a little like playing jazz. You become open, playful, ready to jam this way or that, and without serious limits.

All this took some damn good psychotherapeutic skills of Ken, my weekly rent-a-mom. But I can't help but think that the silence itself, whispering its infinitesimal but steady and playful pull, also had something to do with it. Inner silence doesn't drop into the weeds. But it holds a standard aloft—freedom, no effort whatsoever—and lends a sweetly quiet background tone to a life. It helps keep us going until we are absolutely easy. Be effortless, it says, be absolutely *Wu Wei*. Especially, where you hurt.

One mark of this *Wu Wei* ease around a painful life block is being able to laugh with it. Laughter is a kind of gauge, I think. I knew I was pretty well done with an issue—the ducks, the belt or the others—when I found myself laughing at it. My bet is that this is true for pretty much everyone, but hey, I'm Jewish. When you can't laugh at your troubles or your beliefs or especially your own seriousness, there's probably something that's still got you.

Laughing with them says you're way bigger than your tensions. Kidding around has simply *got* to be part of this!

Gallows humor doesn't count: too bitter. Embarrassed giggling doesn't count either if it means avoidance. Being able to sit with the ridiculous irony of it all is my marker: that you have to go through pain to feel ease, through ease to own your pain, and through both to grow up. How ridiculously ironic is all this?

Standing halfway between dirt and God is, after all, a pretty absurd place to put your sneakers.

A good belly laugh is wide open, when you think about it, navel to throat. To be open-throated like that, feels just the same as does the openness of the silence itself. Where you were hurting and small you get to be big and funny, and the vastness has spread her angel wings.

It and Dragons

I want to tell you one more story. I'm not sure if I want to tell it because it makes a hellova tale (well to me anyway), because it points to a whole other kind of integration that has got to be part of this, or just because it's true. Probably all three.

This one happened a couple of years after I had pretty much worked through that nasty business with my mom. I was forty something by then and my first book, *The Problem of Pure Consciousness,* had just come out. The American Academy of Religion had scheduled a major panel about it for that fall's conference. Dr. Katz and friends were slated to debate the book with me and mine. A friend mentioned with a bit too much concern that Katz said he was "gonna come gunning" for me.

When I first heard that line, I laughed it off as a scholar's gunslinging bluster. But I had encountered this man many times before, and I was afraid of his barbs and innuendoes. You'd have to be "bizarre" to think as I did, he'd once remarked.[69] "Your footnotes are a mess," he'd leveled at me at another conference.[70]

The upcoming meeting was important to me and my young career, and over the next few months I found myself getting more and more churned up. I kept hearing that phrase, "He's gonna come gunning for you." Even when the panel was still nine months away I was waking up in cold sweats!

One night in early April, still an amazing eight months before the conference, I again woke up in the middle of the night, drenched. "This is ridiculous!" I said to myself. I crawled out of bed, put on a robe, and padded out to the living room couch.

Shivering more from fear than cold, I pulled up a blanket. "OK, Bub," I said to myself, "what are you really afraid of here?"

I drew a blank.

"Well, then," I went on, "what's likely to actually happen in New Orleans?"

The echo chamber of my fears switched on: he'll say my

argument about novelty is wrong…He'll ridicule the claim that one does not think... He'll feign wonder…He'll find some inaccurate footnote …He'll say it's bizarre to think this or that.

This was *not* helping.

"OK, OK," I asked myself, taking a deep breath, "beneath all that, what are you *really* afraid he'll say?"

I didn't know. But my breathing had gotten tighter. There was something here. "So tell the truth. What are you *really* afraid of here …?"

Another deep breath: "OK, if I tell myself the real truth, I'm afraid he'll say ……"

"… that I'm *stupid*!"

This one had the thud of truth.

Long pause.

"Yeah, I'm scared he'll say I am stupid."

"Well," I whispered tentatively to myself, "am I? Am I stupid?"

I wanted to leap to my own defense with "of course you're not." But I didn't. After all those years of trying to prove how smart I am, after all my blustering in seminars that I am as quick as the next grad student, after all the A's…here was the moment …

"Yeah," I shuddered to myself, "I could be a *lot* smarter. If I was really smart it wouldn't have taken me nearly so long to see what he was saying and to write my books. I bet I could have done this a whole lot faster! And I know my arguments could be even stronger. I wish I was a *whole* lot smarter. So yeah, truth be told, I *am* stupid."

It was obvious. My breathing loosened a notch, my shoulders let go some. There was indeed something here.

"Well," I went on "I'll bet he'll find some wrong page numbers in some of my footnotes. Maybe he'll say my footnotes are sloppy."

"OK," I wondered, "will he be right? A*re* my footnotes sloppy?"

Again, I didn't particularly want to think this thought. I had tried to get all those notes right, God knows. I'd worked my ass off to get those damn ducks in a row. I've tried to make them perfect. But those ducks did seem to wander off.

"Yeah," I said to myself, "I probably screwed up some of those notes. If he says I'm sloppy, I'd have to say, he'll probably be right! I *don't* have all my ducks in a row."

Even just admitting these things to myself was downright embarrassing. But here it was, the plain old truth. Here was what I was afraid of, stark naked.

"Maybe he'll say that I'm aggressive…

"Well, would he be right?" I asked myself. "*Am* I aggressive?"

This one was actually harder to face. Ever since I could remember I had felt like a victim—of my mother, of my sister, of Proudfoot, now of Katz. I'd built a life around being a victim, and I was staring it in the face. But here it was: maybe I was not just a victim in all this.

I let out another breath, slowly. "You know, now that I think of it, I actually *am* kind of aggressive. Look how I've handled poor Katz. I've probably taken him on in a dozen articles; now a whole book. To him I must seem a damn bulldog! So yeah, I am aggressive. I actually am something of a son of a bitch."

I actually smiled at that one. Maybe I wasn't as much of a wimp and as I'd thought!

For the next half hour, I told myself every scary truth about me I could think of. That I write poorly. That I'd used him to advance my career. That I had co-opted other people's ideas. That I had treated him and his colleagues poorly. Even that I was balding.

I didn't like to think any of these. But the truth was, every nasty thought was in some very real sense true.

At some point I had whispered to myself every dirty, nasty, embarrassing secret I could think of. I had run out of fibs.

At just that moment I looked up. Standing across the room was a huge pot-bellied dragon. Honest to goodness! Green, scaly, slimy, fire-spewing from his nose: a dragon! I could even smell sulfur. And his face was unmistakably, hysterically, Steven Katz's!

Now, I'm not given to apparitions. But this big old pot bellied dragon was so perfect that I laughed right out loud. Katz clearly *was* my dragon. He was dangerous as hell for me. Like St. George I had taken him on. I had made him angry. And I had to slay him.

One thing that made me really chuckle was his pot belly. Katz himself had something of a belly.

Funnily enough, I thought to myself, so do I.

Katz is Jewish, I also saw. And hey, so am I.

He had always seemed pretty aggressive to me. And here I'd just acknowledged how aggressive I was too.

He's a scholar. So am I.

He's smart. So am I.

He edits books, like me. We even both publish with Oxford Press!

And he probably wishes he was smarter…um, just like me.

And there it was. In all the ways I didn't want to think about myself, we were alike. Two Jewish, pot bellied, fire breathing sons of bitches. Katz, my great sulfur spewing dragon, this big old fellow with whom I'd been fighting tooth and nail all these years, was *me*.

He wasn't the one who was spewing venom. It was me. And I am the one with the pot belly!

What I was really afraid of was all the truths about me I couldn't face. That I am aggressive. That I am an angry Jew. That I am a fire-spewing dragon.

It wasn't Katz that I'd been so afraid all these years. It was me!

"*I'm* the bloody dragon," I said out loud.

The very moment I said that sentence to myself, that big, old, slimy, fire-breathing dragon went *zloooop*—like some cartoon character spiraling down a drain—right into my belly. "I'm the effen' dragon" I laughed aloud again. "I'm the one I've been running from!"

I laughed and I cried with the delicious irony of it all! What a bloody hoot!

I got up and danced like some mad Zorba over to where the dragon had been spewing fire. "How perfectly obvious! I *am* stupid! I *am* dumb! My footnotes *are* a mess! I'm the aggressive SOB. Ho dee ho dee ho dee ho!"

No more would I have to run. No more would I have anything to be afraid of. Because no matter what he could think up to say about me—was all *true*!

It actually worked. Never again did I wake up in a cold sweat. Never again did I obsess about Katz, or about any scholar for that matter. Not once.

Oh, I still worked hard to write my arguments and prepare my articles. But the crazy energy, the obsessional echo chamber, simply wasn't any more. St. George had slain his dragon. Which was, of course, St. George.

The November panel in New Orleans turned out to actually be a big deal. The Shootout at the Mystical OK Corral had gotten quite a bit of attention. The room for 150 was overflowing out the double doors; all the biggest names in the field were there. Katz and his mates sat on one side of the podium, Nick Perovich and I from *The Problem of Pure Consciousness* on the other. Everything but the Colt Forty-fives.

He made his points well. But Katz in the flesh wasn't nearly as scary as my dragon had been. When my turn came I offered an analogy. Imagine several rocket ships, each constructed in a different country, in that country's language, of course. Each is affected or shaped by its local culture. But as it leaves earth, each leaves the gravitational pull of its homeland. Like that mystical experiences are the result of someone using language to go beyond their cultural formation, and goes beyond linguistic construction. Each comes to the same unconstructed weightlessness. Different cultures, different language systems, yet all leave the pull of their homeland and come to the same silent, common weightless vastness of space.

Virtually every single question that afternoon was directed at Katz's side of the panel and took off from my rocket ships and weightlessness image. Our new approach was taking hold.

At the end of the event, Ewert Cousins, a well regarded Fordham

Professor of spiritual experience, came up to me, beaming. "Congratulations!" he enthused.

"What for" I asked him?

"At this point," he said, "the field is different. Before today," he went on with a wizened smile, "there was only one acceptable approach to the study of mysticism. Now there are two."

Turns out he was right. Since that day every academic article about a mystic I've seen has begun with an explanation of why the author thinks that the subject's experiences are or are not linguistically constructed or why their cause is or is not in some culturally transcendent source.

This general Katz-Forman debate has by now come to involve hundreds of scholars around the world."[71] I can't help but believe that that dragon zlooping into my belly, and the success of that New Orleans panel, had something to do with it.

The stakes were terribly high for me that day. I was a mere junior scholar, just out of graduate school. A gaff or even a misplaced cynicism could have decimated my young reputation and derailed the whole debate. But I was there, focused, with nary a dragon nor fear in sight. There were no walls over against Dr. Katz that day, little armor. I felt only easiness there with my old dragon. For there was no accusation he could level at me that I hadn't already acknowledged to be true.[72]

God knows I still lie to myself some. I still get nervous about success and failure. I still have truths I can't yet see and issues I don't want to acknowledge. I doubt that we ever get done with shadows.

Nonetheless I can't imagine doing what I do or even sitting here this afternoon quite so undefensively if I was still hiding from too many big truths about myself. If I was still needing to prove how smart I was, if I was still trying to duck my anger, if I was still trying to convince myself that I am right or virtuous or a victim, it would simply be harder to be.

Where we are keeping secrets from ourselves, we have to work hard to not see them. We just can't be loose there, can't possibly play effortlessly. The fear of those very truths and the pain that is hiding from them grips us, holds us back. All that effort to not know becomes part of us, part of our personas, and holds us down into the mundane. Our secrets become our chains into the world.

But bringing all those truths we hide from ourselves into awareness frees us up a good bit. I became towards my dragon and towards what I couldn't allow myself to know precisely as easy as is the silence itself.

It's like we find the ease that is silence in owning our truth. I suppose this is what they mean by the truth will set you free.

I can't help but think that the silence helped me with my dragon that night. Its power was neither obvious nor immediate. But its candle-flame of warmth probably made it just a little easier to venture that next tentative step.

No matter how clearly we know or sense it, the very effortless of silence invites us to that very effortlessness in all things, and it is far easier to acknowledge what is so than to deny it. The Vastness issues a challenge: "Tell the truth. Tell it so completely that there is nothing left to be afraid of. Tell it so thoroughly that there is no room for hidden lies. Tell it so completely that you become effortless."

Silence beckons, ever so slightly, always towards honesty. It challenges us to let go of every lie we tell ourselves. It calls us to conceal nothing, to keep no secrets from ourselves. And then it beckons some more.

"Don't give up," it whispers. "Don't stop until you're *entirely* open. No kidding, don't quit."

That we can have a good belly laugh even when we cry, that we can stare at the scary old truth effortlessly, even when it's embarrassing, that we can do all these at once, is one hell of an invitation.

Enlightenment, the great unmingling of the trans-personal reality *from* the personal, is not the same as enlightenment *into* a trans *and* personal reality. But it is this, I think, that we are — or should be —

after today. It is enlightenment plus. It includes both the effortlessness of inner silence and the ability to jam with abandon, anywhere, everywhere.

I call it "Enlightenment Plus." The plus happens in our everyday life: Jazz in the Soul.

Jazz in the Soul has something to do with *fluidity.* It's being so effortless that we can jam *effortlessly* from painful to serious to laughter to fear to silence and then back again. There are no walls in such a life, no inner resistances. Soul Jazz means you can sink into your own fear and joy and sexiness and vastness and then pop back out again. All in the key of life.

I know no one who lives Enlightenment Plus in every corner of their lives. It is an asymptote. But it's the right asymptote.

Chapter 6

Oft in the World

Sitting next to the stove this morning, I'm struck with how the sensation of warmth merges so indistinguishably with the silence. I feel the wind whistling through my back, as if my body and the room and what is beyond my window is one. I am part of something widespread, gossamer, vast.

There is little between me and the hardness under my feet, the light that blisters across the hermitage floor or the acrid smell of tea steeping on the stove. Nor am I resisting the remnants of sadness I can still feel in my pectoral muscles. Feelings and thoughts and silence and the whistling wind seem to weave together here, thick almost, concatenations of some nearly liquid being. Silence has become stately. And I am no longer so cut off from the world.

Sensing It

The year after that shootout at the mystical OK Corral, I began to research the American grassroots spiritual community. I travelled around the country, met and interviewed dozens of spiritual teachers and adepts, and I slowly felt my way like a blind man towards the picture of today's spiritual world I outlined in *Grassroots Spirituality: What it is, Why it is Here, Where it is Going.*[73]

On one of my trips I was driving north from Oklahoma City on Rt. 35 on a bright summer's morning. I happened to glance over at the ivy growing up the steep highway embankment. It wasn't an especially pretty scene, just a dusty hill, tawny dirt, ivy. I'd seen the like a thousand times.

But I was suddenly overwhelmed by *green*. For no particular reason, olive lime and English Ivy Green registered, really registered. Such a privilege, green! So was the yellow dappling the ivy. And the gritty tan of concrete. And blue overhead, as clear as the Caribbean Sea. And indigo, nearly black, on the western horizon.

That was the first time I fell in love with the world. Since then the brown of oak bark and the day-glo red on a shiny Fire Engine streaking down Broadway have sometimes just bowled me over. The velvety roughness of a pant leg that tickles when you twirl it between thumb and forefinger got me once. So does the feeling in my cheeks as I drive too fast around a country curve. And the gloriously thick sound-texture of Brahms's Third Piano concerto. Once I nearly wept at the mottled grey roughness of the beech tree outside my study window.

A few years later I was on a particularly wet meditation retreat here, crunching down the stone drive here towards the rain-pocking. I found myself utterly entranced by the wispy grey clouds across the way hovering between the hilltops. It was their moist grey mystery that got me. That you can see through a cloud's translucent softness, that straw-green hillsides can emerge like secrets through half-seen clouds, and that dank wooded lanes can be so soggy and puddle-wonderful beneath your sneakers. Isn't the world just delicious sometimes?

I think Maharishi was pointing to something of this in his overly romanticized way when he wrote about a spiritual stage he calls "God Consciousness" in which

> *"the finer and more glorious levels of creation are appreciated...the individual ... experiences waves of love and devotion for the creation..."*[74]

Though his vocabulary still makes me blanch—waves of love and levels of glory? *God's* Consciousness?—I think he catches something of the living magic of these moments.

These moments are quite different than it used to be. I used to pull away, just a little, from color and sound and touch. I had no idea that I was pulling back from the world, mind you; I doubt many do. But my guard was up against the world, constantly, and I just didn't know how to let it down. You cannot teach this kind of thing.

But these openings to color and sound textures mark a whole new level of being in the world. Silence comes to enliven the external world:

> *Ten thousand flowers in spring, the moon in autumn,*
> *A cool breeze in summer, snow in winter.*
> *If your mind isn't clouded by unnecessary things,*
> *This is the best season of your life.*[75]

No doubt all those years of inner work paved the way for these inner-worldly hierophanies. That Oklahoma morning came a few years after I'd worked through the business with my mom, and some years after my pot bellied dragon had zlooped into my torso. Perhaps that work prepared the space for these new mysteries, as if I'd erased some sort of psychic blackboard.

But the dots were not connected in any obvious way. It's not like

I invited in my dragon or worked through those memories and then, *voila:* green! At best it was more of a field-plowing than a sudden seed-sprouting. On the other hand, I know that if I'd been actively *fretting* over some talk I was to give or if I was overtaken with some libidinous fantasy, I would have been way too busy for these ecstasies of green or of clouds. Obsessions clearly can *disallow* this sort of thing, I'm convinced, though not *create* them.

If there's a cause here, I'd have to point once again to 20 years of meditation and to the strangely steadfast expanse that had by now widened like an aura well past my head and shoulders. Perhaps the only place the vastness could continue its slow maturation was outwards, beyond body and mind, into color and light and Brahmsian textures.

It and Ethics

I find myself thinking about ethics this afternoon. Yamana, the kind hearted woman who manages these hermitages, just walked by on her way to the meditation hall. I called to her to remind her that I hadn't yet paid the rent. She smiled and thanked me, told me she'd figure it up, and get back to me. The rent is not much, but it was out there and I didn't want to have to keep reminding myself to remember it.

It was a small act, almost trivial. But it strikes me that if this meditation-silence-soul-jazz stuff doesn't lead us to something of a concern for others, it is narcissism, not wisdom.

Yet the connection is less obvious that we might think. Maharishi used to claim that meditation would lead us to do what was right "naturally." The enlightened would

> *attain a level of life which is the basis of all morality, virtue and right action, and from which [they will spontaneously] fulfill the laws of nature and do justice to all creation.*[76]

The claim was that the enlightened man or woman will "fulfill the laws of nature," that is, will "naturally" do what is right and ethical. Because such a person has transcended self-interest, he or she lives aligned with the energy that sits at the core of the world: the "basis of all morality." Everything such a person does will then be automatically in harmony with the "needs of the cosmos."

> *In the state of enlightenment—and only in this state—actions are fully and automatically in harmony with the needs of the cosmos.*[77]

Even if we disciples could not understand why an enlightened being like Maharishi did this or that, we were sure that everything he did had a mysterious, cosmic rightness to it. For the actions of the enlightened flow out of the core of the cosmos as water flows down a mountainside.

Maharishi was not alone in his claims. Many mystics, I discovered in graduate school, taught that right action grows naturally out of deep mystical transformations. John of Ruysbroeck, for example:

> *"the universal life [is] ready alike for contemplation and for action and perfect in both."*[78]

> *Ethical values arise out of mystical experience, and this experience itself has its source in the One or Universal Self which is the foundation of the world.*[79]

Richard Jones, a scholar of mysticism, wrote:

> *Compassionate action becomes the expression of what [the mystic] is. One is no longer imposing self centered desires through actions. All actions become works for other beings rather than attempts to twist reality to meet the needs of [one's own] illusory independently existing individual self.*[80]

And thus one automatically acts in accord with the deepest needs of the world.

There is another claim behind this one, at least in the East. Hindus and Buddhists believe in Karma, the great cosmic law of cause and effect. Karma says in effect that "what you sow you shall reap." If we act inappropriately today, is the logic, it will just come back to haunt us in this life or the next one. The enlightened, who are able to see or sense the workings of Karma, will thus *naturally* follow it.

But the proof that the mystic or the illumined will naturally do right just wasn't in the pudding. We'd watch some meditator on a retreat who was said to have gained this or that level of enlightenment, and what we saw was underwhelming. They seemed no kinder, no more compassionate and no more ethical than the rest of us *schlemiels*.

And it wasn't only these un-famous meditators. In the 1980's Rajneesh and his organization took some of the millions they got in donations and bought some 100 square miles of Oregon land for an ashram, Rajneeshpuram. Alas within a few years Rajneeshpuram collapsed into bankruptcy, and Rajneesh himself was convicted of embezzlement and tax evasion, and deported.

I think it's fair to assume that he lived in deep contact with the infinite silence. But apparently he was unable to look coolly at his ashram's finances, rigorously manage a budget or even be honest with taxes. Despite some permanent establishment of Brahman, the depth of the Divine, he remained financially careless or dishonest or both.

And this problem wasn't only in the Guru set. We saw financial chicanery among countless western ministers too. The most infamous was probably the flamboyant televangelist, Jim Bakker and his heavily mascara-ed wife, Tammy Faye. During their weekly PTL (Praise the Lord) Club broadcasts, they solicited donations for the Lord's work to great effect. Followers dutifully donated millions. But it turned out that Bakker was embezzling, eventually getting convicted of pilfering some $287,000 to pay for the "parsonage's" air conditioned dog house and gold plated bathroom fixtures. Being born again and charismatic clearly did not provide him with financial rigor (much less good taste!).

The one who really shattered our confidence about the ethics of western ministers however was Jim Jones. Jones wasn't a guru, wasn't even from the East, and to my knowledge never spoke of enlightenment. But by all reports he was a charismatic leader and, I assumed, had developed some level of spiritual attainment.

How then could I make sense of the story that horrified the news in 1978 about his leading some 909 members of his Jonestown, Guyana church to drink cyanide-laced Kool Aide?[81] He induced

276 children to drink the stuff, for God's sake! And simultaneously down the road, his henchmen shot a congressman and four others in cold blood!

No, the claim that mediation and spiritual development would lead to spontaneous right action wasn't at all convincing.

Yet there may be a connection here, if I can tease it out with two stories. The first came about six months after my long retreat. I'm embarrassed to admit this, but even after that silence established itself in my life, I continued to shoplift, one of the more idiotic habits I had begun in college. I had started for kicks, I liked to tell myself, or just to see if I could. But I have to admit that generally what I pilfered was the pricier stuff.

Even half a year after the mystical openness had established itself as my consciousness, I sometimes kept at it. I'd sneak out of a grocery store, my consciousness bottomless, with a wedge of cheese crammed into a coat pocket. I'd skulk out of a bookstore, mystically wide open down my spine, with a paperback beneath my belt.

It was almost laughable. Wasn't this the sort of thing that was supposed to automatically fall away with the permanent "basis of all morality?" Once I walked out of a store, some tasty morsel crammed into a pocket, chuckling to myself, "So much for natural right action!"

Six or eight months after I returned from Mallorca, I hid a box of spaghetti in my gauntlet-length winter glove. I walked out giddy with fear and smugness, a little tickled with myself for having found such a nifty hiding place.

While I was walking home though, I remembered that I hadn't gotten any spaghetti sauce. Or salad fixings. Or dressings for that matter. I hid the box behind a planter a few doors down and skulked back.

Walking up and down those grocery aisles, my heart was seriously pounding. I found myself justifying and re-justifying that little box of spaghetti to myself: "Oh hell, everybody does it." "I'm sure they budget for pilferage." "Why all this fuss? It was just a few cents."

But as I watched myself machinate and self-justify and guilt-deny, it struck me that this was a hell of a lot of energy for a lousy 15 cent box of pasta! Was this really such a great deal?

I lifted another item or two after that. But it wasn't much fun any more. By several months later, I noticed, I had been honest for awhile. No impressive vow to be honest, no weepy confession. I had just stopped.

You can't quite stand up straight when you're skulking, can you? Stopping seemed to have something to do with that. You subtly crouch over, at least inside. Your eyes are always on guard. Even if you're just thinking you might lift something, you sneak. It is hard just to be, and you can't play when you're on guard.

As crime sprees go, this was hardly ten most wanted stuff. It's not like I swore off serial rape or fratricide. But stopping was something. And it happened pretty naturally. It just became obvious: it takes too much work to break the law, even for just 15 cents.

Or for a lot of money either. By ten years later I had inherited a little money from my grandfather. I had put some of it in a Kansas City money market firm, but now wanted to close out the account. So I had the bank send me a check for the full amount, some $27,000. When the statement came the next month though, it said that I still had $27,000.

I thought about that statement for days. I looked at the statement again and again. I kept reciting the monopoly card to myself, "bank error in your favor." I considered calling the bank. Maybe I should withdraw the money a second time? Should I call a lawyer? Maybe I'll have them send it to some charity? At some point it became pretty obvious that fretting about that $27,000 had taken over my life! So I called up the bank and told them about their mistake.

"Oh no sir," said the operator cheerily, "everything's fine."

"But you sent me a check!"

"No, Mr. Forman, it's all in order."

Sheesh! What to do now? I probably could have withdrawn the

money, I knew, though they might figure it out eventually. Calling a second time seemed a little too goodie-goodie. After all, *caveat emptor* points both ways. So, and I'm not saying this was right for everyone, I called a lawyer to be sure I wasn't breaking some law, and decided to just let it sit there.

From that moment on, it barely crossed my mind. I had done what seemed to me to be fair, and I left it in the hands of fate. No more internal debates. No more waking up at night. My life was now my own again.

About six months later, one of their lawyers called me up. "Mr. Forman, Mr. Forman," he began all breathless and urgent. "We sent you a check for $27,000. And then we didn't debit your account!" Even more nervously, "we're going to have to take it back. We're going to need the money"

"I know, I know," I said, chuckling to myself about how long it had taken them. "When I got the statement I called up one of your people and told her. She told me it was all in order." And then without a moment's hesitation I added, "It's yours. Take it."

I could feel the sigh of relief even from 1200 miles away.

Once I had called them to tell them of their mistake, once I had done what seemed to me the decent thing, the whole encounter took absolutely no effort. I hid from no guilt, no second thoughts, and I had no complex feelings to deny. I didn't need to explain or justify anything to him or, more importantly, to myself. Giving it back came out with a chuckle.

I got to keep the interest, by the way, which about covered the lawyer.

As I look back on those two moments, what strikes me is the move towards effortlessness. Shoplifting takes energy, a lot of it. And worry: you can't quite stand up straight, you can't play, when you're doing something you sense is wrong. You can't laugh when you're crouched over inside. And you can't jam when you're trying to hang onto something you know ain't yours.

I suppose choosing to stop lifting, calling the bank back or even calling over to Yamana this morning each took a smidgeon of courage. But they were choices towards ease and the lightness of falling back into what is right for someone else. It's a choice that isn't a choice, really: to be bigger.

I can't but think that the effortlessness of silence played its role here. It was not the automatic "transformation of actions" that aligned with "the basis of the cosmos." But it did and does seem to have its effect. It beckons quietly, towards the less conflicted, towards the smooth, towards what seems right in a larger sense. It invites towards something like the golden rule, I suppose, which leads to effortlessness.

It is easy to miss though. The vastness does not tell us what is right, or not in so many words. There are no "ten commandments of Shunyata (emptiness)." Our desires for money, fame, sex, or even for food at the end of a long day scream awfully loud sometimes. Maybe Rajneesh missed it when he ignored those tax laws.

No matter how much silence we carry though, we still have to decide, and the answers are rarely obvious. Even soaked down to our ankles in a oceanic vastness, we still have to figure out and do the decent thing. The push of silence is more a nudge than a cosmic bludgeon.[82] And even with the cosmic nudge, alas, we can still choose to be an ass or a saint.

Maybe Maharishi was right then, in a sense. It's not like flipping a switch, but the inner openness does exert a slight but constant pressure towards what is right, I think. It is barely there, easy to ignore. But it *is* there, the merest hint, and steady. It nudges always towards truth, towards the utterly unconflicted. And unless one is pathetically narcissistic, that generally includes other people, and points roughly towards the ethical.

It's neither as irresistible nor as unambiguous as I had understood, but in a real and complex world, even a little pressure towards the needs of self and other—towards what is right—is a lot.

And standing up straight with few inner conflicts and doubts, we can play.

The Cloud of Unknowing

Two years after that moment of green on an Oklahoma embankment, I took another week long solo meditation retreat, this time in the gloriously photogenic mountain town of Crestone, Colorado. My final morning there was lovely, so I decided to take the scenic route down to the Denver airport. The mountain roads curved lazily through wide valleys and beneath glacier capped mountains. I put the convertible's top down to watch the glinting peaks slip by.

Perhaps an hour into the drive, the scene began to feel kind of odd. I rumbled to a stop. I looked around at the piney hillsides, over to the ranch house and fields. It was all quite lovely, but nothing unusual.

Then I found myself feeling the scene with something like *peripheral* vision. Yeah, *this* was what was different! There was something—something I could feel more than see—*around* the ranch house and mountains. Some sort of *cloud* was here, all around me and through the valley. It surrounded the split rail fence by the road. It rested between the longhorns grazing on the field and it wafted up the sides of the mountains. Some sort of new openness was here. I could almost touch it, twirl it between my fingers, and sense it wherever I turned. It was even burbling in the stream alongside the road.

At some point I realized that not only was it *around* the mountains and grasses, this whatever-it-was ran *right through* the cattle… It was *inside* the mountains … *through* the whitewashed barn. This hush, velvety and quiet, penetrated everything I could see.

And finally, with a start I realized that it ran right through me as well. "Oh, of course," I laughed to the windshield, "if it's everywhere, it's got to be *in me* too!" The cattle, the fence posts, and the blue of the sky were all the same stuff as me!

The medieval Christian image of a "cloud of unknowing" popped into mind:

> *The higher part of contemplation... consists entirely in this cloud of unknowing, with a loving impulse and a dark gazing into the simple being of God himself alone.*[83]

It *did* seem like this cloud I was gazing into was indeed the "simple being of God himself!" Everywhere I looked I could feel this simple expanse with my chest, belly and legs more than I could see it. But I couldn't possibly have missed it!

An expression of Maharishi's came to mind too: "seeing everything in terms of the self." The mountains, ranch house and road were all the same "stuff" as myself. How perfect, I thought!

This was nothing like the witnessing I'd known by then for nearly twenty years. That unmingling of consciousness from thoughts and sensations was *inside*. This was decidedly *outside*. What I was sensing was yards and miles away, in me but also very much *in* the world.

I got out of the car, leaned on a fence rail and felt into the scene for about half an hour. Cloud through the grasses. Cloud beyond the clear sky. Cloud beneath the valley floor.

When I drove on, I felt strangely settled. Even at 75 miles an hour, I felt like I was it was like watching a dot move on a great map, as if the wind and movement and speed were infinitesimal in this great settled spaciousness.

I pulled into a log cabin restaurant. The mystical is, after all, no substitute for breakfast! Crunching across the parking lot that sense of connection stayed with me, right inside the smells of knotty pine and maple syrup and bacon.

Anne, thirty-something, with big auburn hair and far too much make-up, came to my table, order pad in hand. I looked into her tired, sad eyes. There it was, the same "stuff" infusing through her. I felt amazingly tender towards her, as if I could feel her fatigue and her sadness inside my own chest. She wasn't at all my type, but I swear I could have reached my hand straight into her soul. I had never felt so connected with another human being in my life.

I stared at her, or rather us, no doubt a little too long. She probably thought I was a masher, and a lousy one at that. But I was utterly in love: with her, with the cloud, with the moment. And the pancakes weren't half bad!

I drove down the rest of the way to Denver, the spacious connection remaining beneath me, and dropped my car off at the rental lot. It flowed up to the airport's circus-tent ceiling, below the baggage belt. It spread out down the concourse and billowed under running feet and wheeled suitcases. It was there, inside the airplane wings and through the concrete runway. It even stretched over to the Rockies I could see in the distance.

Evelyn Underhill, grandmother of all mysticism studies, calls this sort of experience the "prayer of union." In it, she writes,

> *The self, though intact, is wholly penetrated – as a sponge by the sea – by the ocean of Life and Love to which he has attained: "I live, yet not I but God in me."*[84]

> *Thou art in me and I in Thee, glued together as one and the self same thing.*[85]

Meister Eckhart describes this as being indivisibly connected with the "ground of the Godhead."

> *This ground is an impenetrable stillness, motionless in itself, and by the immobility all things are moved, and all those receive life that live of themselves...*[86]

In Maharishi's frame I was experiencing a few hours of "unity consciousness," in which the seer and the seen

> *are together in perfect oneness, in the oneness of absolute unity. Then he and (the infinite silence) are one in himself. Then :.. [he sees everything] in terms of himself.*[87]

Later that afternoon, waiting for my airplane to board, I began to feel like I was *trying* to hold onto it. That was, no doubt, a sure sign it was fading. With so little protective armor against all those people in the Denver airport, I found myself getting ever so slightly afraid. It drifted away like a fragrance.

For many years I didn't tell a soul about that day. I thought about it a lot though. It was an interesting if temporary step forward.

If I tell the real truth here, I was probably a little tickled with myself for having such a cool unitive vision. Spiritual experiences often do that — well, they do it to me anyway. "I've had a moment of unity consciousness" is not the kind of thing you say out loud to a friend or even to yourself. But you feel it as a cock of the head, a slightly smug smile. I suppose that this sort of self-puffing was part of what I was afraid to lose that afternoon. It's easy to think you're all egoless and don't cling to what happens to you, but these things have a way of sneaking in, don't they?

Nonetheless being a guy that once spent a day in a cloud of unknowing counts for very little in the daily grind of teaching classes, just-missed subway doors or the slicing of broccoli. After a few months the whole thing — the feeling, the memory, the vanity — faded.

Even so, as I think about it now, it *was* remarkable. Though I had risen to a possibility I couldn't long sustain, that was my first experience in which the spaciousness I had known so many years *inside* had widened beyond my own body to the *outside,* into the world. And where it was pointing during those eight hours was, I think, someplace real. We *are* connected, way down deep. We do all live within a single space, maybe within a single quantum field. Perhaps we share a single consciousness. Whatever it was and however brief, it was a kind of gift, and I am grateful.

It was not to be the last. About six months later I was watching the New York City Ballet. Again, with no particular cause, that oceanic cloud suddenly descended into Lincoln Center. It flowed through the backs of the purple velvet seats, the bald heads, the mink shawls. It filled the whole New York State Theatre. It was inside as well as out there; I could almost touch it.

This time however it seemed to move, or rather be movement. Ballet dancers have always amazed me, but this time I could feel each one moving fluidly within this cloud, as if she or he was inside my own torso. I could feel one leap through my chest. When she bowed, I felt her deep in my belly. The *pas de deux* was in both sides of my ribcage. I enclosed them all: stage left, right, front and rear. They were *in here, in* the cloud, in me, far more clearly than they were up there.

After perhaps a half an hour, it faded. Once again I was eyes only. But it was easily the most enthralling performance I'd ever experienced. This was getting interesting.

The Peculiarly Spiritual Life

I doubt that the path ever ends. I didn't used to know this.

In my line of work, I've met a lot of wise spiritual souls. I've had long talks with more than a thousand, I'd bet. But I've yet to meet anyone who is truly free, lives soul jazz in every domain. Some come across as peaceful but are covertly withdrawn and afraid. Some come across as sociable but secretly avoid being alone. As Jung put this:

> *I cannot possibly tell you what a man who has enjoyed complete self-realization looks like, and what becomes of him. I never have seen one.*[88]

We can come pretty close to freedom in several life-domains. But we can always become freer in some areas, if we keep at it, though the process is more humbling than we like to acknowledge and calls for mastering wider skill sets than we expect. Effortlessness in each domain represents its own kind of mastery, and we do not become multi-capacity wizards through any one set of skills.

Yet in one arena, the shift in our relationship to objects, there really are a few singular leaps. Consciousness really does shift in structure. It may mature slowly, like an electron increasing in energy, but at some point there comes a leap, sudden and whole. I cannot imagine missing it. You really do become a different kind of being. And it is not insignificant. A transubstantiated consciousness really does change things in quiet and long term ways. Indeed this may be *the* core change.

But again, and this is the discovery that took so many years, it does not change everything. You can shift your consciousness and still be anxious or foolish or silly or sad. An existential shift is not a personality transplant. By itself it just is not enough.

What is enough is a lifetime of multi-hued transformation. Learning to live the jazz that marks the free soul—deep and wide, horizontal and vertical—the *telos* for our complex age, takes determination and a whole toolbox. Finding these tools is part of our life's work.

To the extent that we sense it, silence may be a strange attractor in all this. It is so very unassuming, yet so very insistent. You fight it and you disbelieve it and you struggle to disprove it. But once present, it simply remains.

"You are trying too hard," it hints. "You do not walk with me here."

You ignore it, you long to become famous or rich or beloved, and still it remains, beneath your feet, unbowed. You work and you scheme and you fantasize and you hope. And all it does is whisper: "Be. Flow. Simple."

If you're lucky, you learn haltingly to stand up fairly straight in it, silence in your spine, and play.

And then it calls you again.

Chapter 7

It in Relationships

Buddha Alone in It

It snowed again last night. A heavy drift blew up the Locust tree, nearly covering the little Buddha at its base. Only his head pokes out of the snow bank this morning, like some crowning newborn. His topknot and curls stand out regally. He looks especially content there so alone.

He's always alone, now that I think of it. You never see "Buddha and Wife." You never see him in a group.[89] St. Francis is always shown alone with his birds, though I hear that as a youth he was quite a flirt. Sikh founder Guru Nanak is always painted alone, even though he was married to Sulakhani and was the father of two. Why is the spiritual journey always taken alone?

Is this really such a good idea? Think about a fellow like Ramana Maharshi. At the age of 16 he laid himself down on the floor of his bedroom, crossed his arms in the death pose, held his breath, and pretended to have died. "If my body dies," he says to himself in a fit of astonishingly bad metaphorical reasoning, "something remains." So to find "that which remains" he grabbed the few Rupees he had, hopped a train to Mt. Tiruvanamalai, and found a secluded meditation spot in the shade of a Hindu temple. There he remained for months on end, clad only in a loin cloth, deeply alone.

He survived by India's custom: passers-by respectfully left bowls of food and water for the nearly naked holy boy. He remained within a few miles of that temple for the rest of his life, living on India's veneration of its silent sages, and eventually came to be regarded as a *mahapurusha,* a "great being." I have no doubt that he found the Self beyond the self, the formless Brahman, and that he became a great guru.

Yet despite the progress he made as a silent sage-boy and later as a guru, because of his life choices he missed some enormous spiritual opportunities, I think. He never held a job, so he never had to learn to answer an angry boss. Once the ashram grew up around him, he became its absolute dictator. (Nice gig!) He had "devotees," but no peers. That means that not one person ever really questioned, doubted, squabbled with, or even gently confronted him. He never had to work out a difference with a wife or even a college dorm-mate, not once. He never negotiated a deal or even decided on a room layout with somebody else. His opinion was *never* questioned.

It was a charmed life. But such charm leaves some huge lacunae. When I lived for half a year in Benares, India, I was befriended by a "*mahant*," the spiritual leader of a Hindu Temple, a role much like a guru. Except for foreigners, he once confided to me, there was no one with whom he could have a personal relationship. Every seeming friendship was shot-through with status differences and implicit requests. Only with foreigners like me could he just talk or think aloud, he said, and not have to worry about consequences. He could only be himself with someone outside his system.

A guru like Ramana lived in even more of a bubble. Even the outsiders who came to visit him were potential devotees. That means that he probably never had a single peer to peer friendship.

Nor did he ever marry. He no doubt died a virgin. No one ever asked him to articulate a feeling he did not know he felt or make himself even slightly vulnerable. No lover ever jilted him. And no one, not one person, would dare to even hint that he might be wrong or foolish or just the teeniest bit blind to his own motivations.

Ditto for the great Christian mystics. Once Athanasius, St. Benedict, St. Frances, St. Theresa, Meister Eckhart or even Mother Theresa of Calcutta had become renowned saints, people tended to look at them fairly doe eyed, and to hang on every word. Their decisions, wise or foolish, and their blindnesses also went largely unchallenged.

What would such a context do to a psyche? How would one learn to be intimate, to deal with conflict, to confront adversity? What or who would challenge such a person to keep stretching beyond his or her comfort zone or cultural assumptions? How might he or she learn to deal with some catty office mate or with a challenging budget (here think Rajneesh)? As Pir Vilayat Kahn, head of the Sufi order in the West, once put it:

> *of so many great teachers I've met in India and Asia, if you were to bring them to America, get them a house, two cars, a spouse, three kids, a job, insurance, and taxes...they would all have a hard time.*[90]

Modern lives are just complicated! Though we live in apartments and houses right next to each other, we neither dress, believe nor think alike. We talk every day with people of the opposite sex, who may disagree with us, and they may (occasionally) be right! If we live in a big city, we talk every day with people whose native language is Spanish, Swedish, Japanese or English. We hang out with Christians, Jews, Hindus, Buddhists, and with folks who are lapsed from each. On the bus we stand very close to, and are jostled up against, lots of others, some of whom are our spiritual path-mates, most of whom are not.

When you and I meditate, alas, no one puts bowls of food in front of us. So we have to get up from our cushions and go earn a living. In ancient times we'd have to plow the fields or tan the hides. Today we have to commute to the office, fix the car and pay the gas bill. Some of us have to wake up night after night to rock a colicky baby. We all get called on our foolishness and, if we're smart, grow from it. Even if we're CEO's and in charge, our decisions rarely go unchallenged. And we often do have to work out with others what color to paint the bedroom, where to spend the income, and maybe which religion in which we'll enroll the children.

Many spiritual seekers and teachers long ago and today have been married or in seriously committed relationships. And as it turns out, we're not especially good at it. Virtually every spiritual teacher that I know personally—and I know quite a few—has gotten *at least* one divorce. That's in America, Canada, England and Sweden. There is no study yet, but my sense is that the odds for staying happily married are no better among serious spiritual teachers and seekers than average. Very possibly worse!

I'm thinking of this today because my friend Jen, who leads wonderful retreats to Egypt and India, emailed me yesterday that she just left her husband of 15 years. "Honestly," she emailed simply, "he could never understand me." Nikki, college botany professor, just left my spiritual facilitator friend Tom and their 18 month old child. Since their separation four months ago, my spiritual psychologist friend Rita hasn't been able to say anything nice about Teddy, her husband of 18 years and father of her three. Nathan, a spiritually oriented professor, was married for one very intense year and a half: "too many energy clashes" was his phrase. And I think of Ethan, a wise Presbyterian minister and a dear friend who's still married after two decades. But he and his wife neither really talk nor have sex, and he complains to me often about it all.

Wonderful people, excellent facilitators, yoga teachers and preachers all. But when I think about the spiritual goal that's right for today, surely this *can't* be it!

Psychiatrist and student of mysticism Arthur Deikman offers what he half jokingly calls his "spiritual leaders' test." It has only one question: "How are they with their spouse?" As a group we are failing.

Gautama Buddha faced the challenge of freeing himself and escaping the clutches of the demon, Mara, with inspiring courage. But let's face it, he summarily left Yasodhara, his wife, and Rahula, his son, thereby committing history's first recorded spousal abandonment. Never again would he face the spiritual challenge that is intimacy. What would he have done—no really, what *would* he have done—if Yasodhara, or any Mrs. Buddha, asked him,

"Where do you really hurt inside, Gautama dear?"

Honestly, I can't imagine what he would say. In all the Pali Buddhist literature, I don't know a single passage that describes how, after his night of enlightenment, he had an honest-to-goodness moment of doubt or even a regular old human emotion. Or where he acknowledged even the teensiest shortcoming. [91]

"Tell me, dear Sakyamuni, where you are tender? Do you have even a vague feeling?" Could he name even a single second in which he felt inadequate—to himself, to her, to his people's yearnings? Universal love is nice and all, but could he name a specific moment of enjoyment? Did he ever dance?

And what would he say if she asked, as Yasodhara very well might have, "You love all people, Gautama dear. Do you love *me* in any special way?"[92]

Conversely, what would some modern Yasodhara say if he told her, as the tradition had it, that she could only gain the exalted state of Nirvana by becoming a male? Would she calmly accept it, and with it his barely concealed claim to marital dominance? What self-respecting woman of today would stay? And if she walked out in fury, would his hands stay folded so primly?

And if they did, would that be such a good thing? Given what we know today about human emotion, is such invulnerability really what we want? To be able to sit in detached and preternatural calm, with love for all beings, may be an escape from the real challenge.

Real everyday life, especially life in relationship, is just more complicated, and more interesting. Jack Kornfield, in his wonderfully self-critical *A Path with Heart*, describes coming back from his years in an Asian Buddhist monastery. Although he returned from the monastery, he says,

> *clear, spacious and high, in short order I discovered, through my relationship, in the communal household where I lived, and in my graduate work, that my meditation had helped me very little with my human relationships. I was still emotionally immature.*[93]

Me too. By the early nineties I had come to understand silence and had woven much of it into my own personal psyche. But doing so was not enough. I was still too cut off, too introvertive within myself. Only if I could somehow learn to live the ease of enlightenment within and through my marriage, my friendships and all my relationships, I thought, might it be enough. But what would it mean to live enlightenment plus *within* relationships?

It in a Group

This question was in the back of my mind in 1995, when I arranged a meeting of "spiritual activists" in St. John the Baptist Retreat Center, Mendham, NJ. I had invited a dozen spiritual leaders and teachers from around the US and Canada to a weekend of "Exploration across our Differences." We had invited the proverbial rabbi, priest and minister, plus a Vajrayana Buddhist teacher, a Siddha Yoga chant leader, a transpersonal psychologist, another TM teacher and so on to explore not our well-known differences but what we might all have in common.

I had planned the weekend in typical academic conference style: 20 minute papers and 10 minutes of Q & A. Susan read hers first. We applauded politely.

Then Rachel, our resident transpersonal psychologist, got up. She looked at her paper. She looked at us. Then she said, "you're such wonderful people. I don't want to read you a paper. I just want to tell you my story."

And she did. She told us about her spiritual breakthroughs at Eselen. She cooed over what she'd been learning from her daughter. She wondered aloud about how to bring more spiritual depth to her therapy clients.

It was just right! So we all tossed our papers and with our half hours slots, told one another who we were. We shared about our spiritual lives. We talked about where we each felt confident and where uncertain.

And we described what it was like for us to find the divine. When Marius told us of his birding walks in Northern California, we could almost feel his tentative footfalls on the forest floor, hear the Towhees calling from deep in the woods and sense the sacred in the pine needles. When Nancy told us of her first experience with Jesus in the Cathedral of St. Paul, I could swear I smelled frankincense. Tim described an evening when, at seven, the stars and the sky overhead swirled into a great cosmic unity, and how's he's struggled to paint it ever since.[94] Many had never before known anyone with whom they could share these stories, and they were grateful. We laughed. A few of us cried. Sometimes it felt as if the walls and floorboards had fallen away.

Saturday evening came. Howard was the last to share. He told us how he hoped to live up to the example of his Tibetan guru and his struggles to make his Texas Vajrayana Buddhist center financially viable.

Dusk was settling in as he finished. We placed a few votive candles around the room. I whispered, "I have something to say."

I didn't know quite what I wanted to say. But I knew that something was bubbling up. Some important doorway had been opened. With a little time in stillness with those people, I could feel, whatever needed to be said would come through.

Everyone waited. No one giggled. No one fidgeted; no coughing. Twelve people in a circle, poised in the kind of patient respectfulness that comes only after real truths have been shared. Three, maybe five minutes …

It didn't matter that we hailed from different paths. It didn't matter that some of us were secular and some religious. The only thing that mattered was that we had come to trust one another and become simple together, and that we had found each another in the space beneath our brokenness.

"I have never had the privilege," I whispered, "of being in silence with people who are on different paths than mine, yet who value quiet as much as I do."

Nods.

More silence.

Rachel appreciated how honest we had all been. Bill noted that over the years we had all struggled, and yet had kept the faith.

More nods.

Quiet again.

It was only a few moments, the shadows of the forest settling deeper into our little room. Yet to be in that circle was to be surrounded by mystery, and to open out past our walls towards the pond below the hillside and beyond towards the ocean to the East. It was to sit together in deep mutuality, eyes open, and hardly to breathe …

We had each encountered the infinite in our lives, whether we had called it God, Brahman or the Mystery. We were all spiritual ministers or writers or teachers. But these encounters had generally been private affairs, even when surrounded by church or temple throngs.[95] Robert, our resident Zen Buddhist, thought of these moments as *satoris,* breakthrough experiences, and they always came to him alone on his zafu cushion. To Jesuit Father Richard, such life shattering "experiences of the Divine" had come while in chapel with other people, but always within his own breast, he said. To Andy, our resident Taoist, the opening came with downcast eyes while doing his slow moving Tai Chi k*atas.*

But the opening that happened that Saturday evening at Mendham was *in* no one of us. This came to us together, eyes open, in and through all of us, collectively. We had talked. We had laughed. And together, with love and respect, we had a *mutual* mystical moment.

Even today, describing that time, I am struck with how much we broke through that weekend. We stopped our habitual theorizing *about* the sacred. We dropped beneath our customary posings and spoke real truths about who we were. Most of all, we broke through the ancient pattern of encountering the mystical only alone. We pushed through to the liminal as a group.

Since that weekend I have heard of others who have encountered the mystical in mutual moments. Many speak of finding it in relationship[96]. But to every one of us, what happened that evening at Mendham was something new.

The next day we offered different descriptions of what we'd fallen into together. To Rachel it was the "transpersonal reality." To Rabbi Harold it was the *shechina, the* female divine principle. It was Christ consciousness. It was *shunyata,* the Buddhist emptiness.

It was *Atman*.

Different words splaying back to different whole traditions. But what was below was the same felt vastness. It was as if we had each wandered down from our respective mountains and splashed together into the same wide and still valley waters.

Just for those few moments we broke through to the sacred in a whole new domain: the mutual, the interpersonal. The sacred had emerged into our midst.

Since those days, we have coined the term "trans-traditional" for such mutual mystical contact. That is, what we encountered together was the "*trans*cendent." Yet we hailed from different *trad*itions: thus "trans-traditional." Right there, across history's most ancient divisions, the transcendent revealed itself to us collectively. The late Wayne Teasedale called it the "Interspiritual."

For all their brilliance, Ramana Maharshi, St. Benedict or the Buddhist Nagarjuna simply could not be aware of such a possibility. They did not have access to the full range of the world's religions. And given their more stratified societies, few had occasion to sit in a circle of their peers, much less peers from other religious systems. Even Meister Eckhart, who had considerable mastery of Jewish and Arabic philosophies, probably never chatted with a living Muslim or sat down with many actual Jews in his native Cologne. Nor did any of them leave behind a single sentence about a struggle or a confusion they may have had (and it's hard to believe that not one of them never had, even if only subconsciously, a teeny-weeny conflict or doubt).[97] And certainly no tradition has left us descriptions of a comparable out-loud, trans-traditional mystical moment.[98] As a scholar I have read and heard endless accounts of religious or spiritual experiences; to me this was new.

We came together again six months later, this time to Kathy's rambling ranch house near San Antonio, Texas. Again the sharing of struggles. Again the whispering of secrets. Again mutual explorations.

Sarah stole the show this time, mulling aloud whether she should fly to Italy to become mistress to her sexy Italian boyfriend or to Seattle to become a full time minister. Really! (I was rooting for the boyfriend. She went for the collar.)

And just as we had at Mendham, sometimes during prayers, after someone dropped into some new discovery, or when Jonas blew his breathily mysterious Shakuhachi flute, we found ourselves together again in that deliciously effortless spaciousness. Again, mutual mysticism.

This was the same divine openness that had found me many years before. Of this I had no doubt. I believe that it was the same spaciousness to which we had all dedicated our lives. But again this wasn't within any of our breasts or *from* any one of our traditions but in and through us all. And it took nary a hint of effort to fall into it.

I'm not sure why our little circle was able to open this particular sluice-gate. Being on our respective paths for 20 or 30 years no doubt helped. So did our personal acquaintance with such a space. Sharing our confusions and our secrets, letting down our defenses, all must have helped set the stage.

But other groups did these things too, I knew. I could only think that some sort of grace was involved here as well, though I still can't say just what that means. All I can say is that, in some way well beyond our control, we dropped together into that space of "a wholly different order." And then we did it again.

This was so much fun and so important that at the end of the San Antonio weekend, folks said they wanted to help shape the Forge Institute, the organization that we had by then incorporated to promote whatever had manifested in our midst. So six months later we flew to a retreat center outside New Orleans.

The question for the weekend was, what should the Forge become? We began by opening the floor to suggestions.

"Let's host more retreats like these," said one, excitedly.

"Let's develop a new theology to account for all this," offered our theologian.

"How about buying a piece of land and building a 'trans-traditional' retreat center?"

"A network of small groups?"

"Write a book... "

"Start a journal…"

"Host dialogues on TV…"

All sincere suggestions. All interesting ideas. But all *different.* And soon it was,

"Retreat center?? You've gotta be *crazy* to think we have that kind of money!"

"A new theology? Get off it! Who reads theology books anymore? You're stuck in old Catholic thinking!"

"Oh come on! Conferences every six months are just too infrequent. They won't open people deeply enough."

"Who the hell needs another book??"

And with furrowed brows and rising voices, we were eviscerating the very miracle that was our reason for being.

We were all a little stunned that we'd gotten so bollixed up. After all, we'd each been on our paths for decades. We'd all let go our cravings and unhooked our stuck places. We'd even taught meditation and helped others let go of their stuck places. We were *spiritual teachers*, for god's sake!

But there it was, or rather wasn't. Despite our best attempts at reconciliation, by the end of the weekend we were working to paste over our differences, and our effortless openness was nowhere to be found. Beneath the clashing opinions and interpersonal tensions, we had destroyed the very trans-traditional magic for which we were together.

We knew how to look each other in the eye. We knew how to tell deep truths and open our hearts. But when resources and money and time were at stake, apparently we had no idea how to disagree and remain that open.

This turns out to be more common than I knew. I've told this story a few times since those days, and I've often heard another tale just like it: the church that's dedicated to love and brotherhood but whose board members cannot stand each other. The spiritual group that teaches about cooperation, but whose members can't come to a simple decision. The Zendo that has ossified in power struggles.

No matter how advance is our inner development, when there's money and resources and time at stake, we spiritual and religious adepts seem to be rank beginners. Either we tend to suppress discussion in paroxysms of obedience to the guru, into painfully inefficient attempts at consensus, or we just don't get along.

This is one of the dirty little secrets of the spiritual and religious worlds. Though our paths and teachers offer profound teachings and tools, few of us know how to work well with others, *unless we ourselves are in charge*. Masters we may be, but masters of mutual cooperation we are not.

The depths of silence, the wonders of openness, do not teach us to play well with others.

Well why? Ken Wilber distinguishes three domains in which we live and do our work: the I, the We and the World (or the personal, the collective and the external).[99] To bring about a change in one realm, he suggests, does not necessarily bring about a change in the others. You can discover a profound connection with God but still remain shy, tongue tied or bossy with others. Conversely, you may be friendly or a hellova listener, yet never introspect to your hidden impulses or discover the expanse of silence. And many of us ruminative types have terrible antennae for the emotional tone of a group. The I and the We require different skill sets.

The folks that came to Mendham were masters, more or less, of the I, of the solo spiritual path. We were a pack of lone wolves, if you will, leading our respective flocks into our respective wildernesses.

We were specialists in the solo because it's what we learned from our traditions. The St. Bonaventures and Ramana Maharshis of the world left us tools and guidance to discover God solo , not in groups, and certainly not in diverse groups. And so we have worked towards, and found, our illuminations solo.

But this is no longer enough for us. When we see people from other traditions in every bus and restaurant, we know in our bones that we must learn to live and work across sometimes difficult divides. We know that to be fully open today, in our multi-cultural world, we must learn to love, work and to make decisions with folks like and unlike us as effortlessly as we do anything else.

As Martin Buber said, the inability to encounter each other as truly autonomous others, and to develop answers in the spirit of genuine contact even with folks who are different,

> *is not only the most acute symptom of the pathology of our time, it is also that which most urgently makes a demand of us. I believe, despite all, that the peoples in this hour can enter into ... genuine dialogue [where] each of the partners, even when he stands in opposition to the other, heeds, affirms and confirms his opponent as an existing other. Only so can conflict certainly not be eliminated from the world, but be humanely arbitrated and led toward its overcoming.*

How to play will with (diverse) others is *the* spiritual question, if not the *primary* question, for our era. And it doesn't come from the silent vastness. Somehow the *telos* for our era, the complete enough enlightenment, will have to include playing well, working well, living well, with others.

As I drove away from that disappointing New Orleans weekend, I found myself wondering if it was even possible. We can meditate and find God within. We can tell each other real truths. We may even be able to find an effortless vastness in our midst for a few precious moments. But to be open with other people, even when there's skin in the game and decisions to be made—is this even possible?

It in Duet

We spiritual types are very good at alone. Alone is, like the little Buddha outside my hermitage, where we untangle some of our confusions and drop into depth.

But alone, down in our Buddha-bellies, is also a hellova place to hide.

Those moments of mutual mysticism, drew me on like a perfume. I didn't know why back then. Perhaps I sensed in them part of an answer to my own longstanding fears and loneliness. Perhaps bringing spiritual leaders and teachers together seemed like part of the answer to our centuries of religious misunderstanding and conflict. Perhaps I was expressing something of our times. But I think those magical seconds offered another promise as well, deeper and to me more surprising: another domain for enlightenment to flow into, a whole new form of awakening. Whatever it was, there was something here; I could smell it.

Thus began The Forge Institute, a community whose calling was to tease out this new level of Being, to learn and perhaps to teach how to be together in deep truth across traditions. We cooked up a Board. We we introduced it to interested folks through a series of one on one phone calls.

That's how I was introduced to Corena, a high spirited and insightful psychologist, facilitator and meditation teacher from Washington, DC. Within the first five minutes of our introductory conversation, we found ourselves laughing giddily over how many people we knew in common. Then, as if we'd both flipped a switch, we suddenly went serious. I told her about the grace of those moments at Mendham. She told me of a similar connection beneath words that she'd found with some of her therapy clients. I shared a dream. Then laughter again. It was deep and insightful and funny and surprising in a way that had us both a little off balance.

Two months later, in Washington on other business, we actually met, sitting on the terrace outside an Indian restaurant, watching people window shop on DuPont Circle. She told me how excited Eve, her four year old, had been about frying up her first potato pancakes. I told her about making matzo balls with Hannah, my niece. She reflected on her longings as a mother. I wondered aloud about my confusion about being The Forge's founder, a paradox which I had not been consciously aware. We shivered in the evening chill. We laughed. And we filled napkins with kitchen layouts and recipes and a diagram of Beck and Cowan's spiral of human development.

We met again a few months later in New York. She named tensions with her sister she hadn't understood. I got to rethinking my own jealousies and wondered aloud about the spiritual goal. She spoke of how she sometimes hid behind her role as a psychologist. We could explore anything, feel anything, without resistance. There openness between us was remarkable, like a heart beating from beneath the table between our elbows.

When I'd tell her something I hadn't realized before, she'd whisper "wow," and I'd feel utterly seen. When I fed her back to her, she told me, she saw herself as more intelligent than she knew. I offered her her, and she me.

To sit across from Corena, or to watch tears well up in her eyes, was to be more awake than I was used to. And the feeling was mutual. Bumping into each other as we walked down Connecticut Ave., ducking into a Buddhist antique shop, laughing at the ridiculous giddy irony of it all: for the first time I knew what it is to be with another human being with virtually no friction. It was a gift.

Our circle at Mendham had alerted me to the possibility of being in a vastness together. That was a few minutes, a weekend. But here was effortlessness, mutual, fresh and unprocessed, week after week. It happened through some miracle of personal chemistry, spiritual training and good luck. But whatever the cause, this was an effortless spaciousness that was mutual, out loud, between, and for months. Flowing with her was more like ice skating than ice skating.

It was platonic love and loss and laughter and frustration and depth and non resistance at 200 miles. Freedom here came through the quality of our being together. It wasn't *inside* either of us but *between*, in the *relationship* itself.

The sacred was now erupting into real life, out loud, with words and tears and can't-catch-breath laughter.

But it had to end. Such a relationship was as impossible as two otherly-married people can be. More deeply though, it had to end because neither of us had any idea how to keep the openness, the non-resistance, from evaporating when things got dicey, as they would, inevitably, and did.

The key that opened the door to long term effortless came from one Douglas Kruschke. An energetic, fast talking and thoughtful Los Angeles corporate consultant, Doug was as interested in mutual mysticism as I was. But his years as a corporate facilitator has taught him how to make relationships themselves part of the path.

Even long term, and even when there's a hard decision to be made, he claimed, relationships *can* give rise to the kind of spaciousness we had found at Mendham. The trick is to make the way we are together as deeply straight, above board and open as is the Vastness itself.

I doubted it. I'd seen some pretty decent relationships in my life, especially recently, but I had never known one with the kind of ongoing, unhesitant trust and openness he was describing. It was no doubt due to my own limitations, but all my friendships and even my love relationships had always ended up in some degree of self protection and distancing. Despite moments of openness, I'd never known a long term relationship that had remained truly spacious.

Yet as Doug and I talked Saturdays week after week, literally hundreds of hours of conversation, it was striking how effortless it was becoming. We both remarked how easy it was to flow from the Forge to football games to spiritual wisdom to investment strategies to foolishness and then back again. It was *surprisingly* effortless. We wondered, we argued, we pondered — about God, life, gender, mysticism and the Lakers versus the Bulls. Perhaps others are more used to this sort of free connection, but I for one had never seen conversation after conversation with so few walls.

On and on we went, month after month of conversations. This mutual openness was truly long lived in a way those wonderful moments in Mendham or with Corena could not be. Here, long term, was exploration with almost no forbidden territories. And we laughed a lot.

A year after we'd first talked, Doug told me he wanted to "bump our relationship to the next level." Clearly enjoying the mystery of whatever that meant, he flew to New York for the weekend.

For three days we told each other where our connection had been easy and where it had been hard. We named where we had spoken complete truths and where we had hidden something. Little by little, we talked through our purpose in being together, and typed out something about "the largeness of Being that inspires us each to grow" and "the fun of stimulating each other's ideas and of creating something together."

We soon found ourselves talking about where things went well and where not in our and other relationships. I told him about a friend who often made promises that he didn't keep. It was trivial stuff mostly, showing up 15 minutes late for meetings, not calling when he said he would, not responding carefully to drafts. Such little acts mess up my schedule and together become irritating as hell. Every time he breaks a promise, I said, I have to work it through. I can handle any of them, I told Doug. The problem is, I have to. So we agreed that that we would make clear promises and keep them meticulously. (It's helped!)

Then we got to discussing what we wanted to do when we got stuck, upset with each other or all jammed up. I still like what we wrote:

At times of stuckness, I will:

go beneath the initial level of my understanding of my motivations and feelings to discover things that free us.

Let you know what I agree with and appreciate about your point before focusing on what I disagree with, or going on to make my own point.

Act as if I am 100% responsible in this stuckness.

Look for how I contributed to things being where they are and how I am responsible for my reactions to what has occurred, especially in regard to any upsets I experience.

We talked through every hard issue we could think of, how we'd try to make decisions, that we'd celebrate our little successes, anything that might help our being together. When we were done we lit a fire in my fireplace and read them out loud to each other like we meant it, lending it a formal flourish I liked.

I must say, that weekend, those agreements, have helped us remain clear, close and open, now more than a decade and a half of wondering, disagreeing, arguing, pondering and laughing.

There is a kind of corporate feel to writing down such rules; Doug was, after all, corporate. Nonetheless co-creating this document and witnessing its effect has been a revelation. We transformed a friendship that had serendipitously manifested the sacred into one whose mutual flow we could count on. We hashed out tools and agreements that actually helped maintain the sacred flow between us. We created a friendship whose flow we could *depend* on, even when we got jammed up, a relationship that was itself sacred. And long term.

I had known those short-lived "peak" moments of openness or pure consciousness in the early days. I had seen it aloud with others at Mendham and recently with Corena.

But in writing down these agreements, in making it conscious and intentional, we made it possible to live and work and laugh in openness with something approaching *permanence*, just as the silence inside had become permanent. We created something like an enlightened relationship, a friendship and colleagueship whose very process is consistently free, pretty undefensive and open.

Interestingly our agreements weren't about us as individuals. None of our agreements focused on inner feelings, the personal or even spiritual states. The openness we protected that weekend had to do with *telling* truths, taking responsibility *aloud* for our role in upsets, keeping whatever is *between* us clean. Sacred experiences may be, but sacred relationships aren't about what we feel inside. They have to do with how we act and talk and dance together. The sacredness of a relationship is *between*, not *within*. What happens inside, inner feelings or silence or whatever, are always in there, of course. But in this domain enlightenment is expressed in how we are together, in the *inter*-personal.

We'd found another way for enlightenment to "jam" in the world, and important one. It's not within us but manifests in the in-between, in how clean are the interactions themselves. Enlightenment plus in an *us*.

It's mastery of a different color.

It in a Marriage

Ok, the obvious issue. I had tried to be spiritual with Yvonne. I had worked to let my openness have its effect on her. I had tried to drop into that space of deep connection with her, as I had at Mendham and the ballet. I had tried to accept her, to be tolerant of who she was. When we'd argue, I'd work to find the spaciousness and to include her in it. But frankly, we weren't doing very well.

We'd certainly had our good times—kids, trips, vacations, discussions. But during 25 years of marriage Yvonne and I had never stopped struggling: about theology, about cleaning the counters, about who would pick up the kids. We tangled over investments, bedroom colors, which house to buy. And in comparison to what I had worked through with Doug, we were lousy at resolving our issues, much less "kicking it up to the next level." We had compromised, we had coped (which meant that neither of us got what we really wanted) and we had learned to not express our unresolved issues, systematically turning them into buttons too hot to touch.

Then there was the personal stuff. She felt excluded. I felt judged. She wanted respect, I wanted to be seen for who I was. And we had cleaned up little of it.

As Issue after issue got consigned to relationship purgatory, we had pretty well lopped everything out of our relationship but politics, the children and food. (And god forbid I should take the wrong political stance!) The rest of our lives were ruled out. I felt like a twelve cylinder car firing on three. I'm sure she did too.

"My life is dedicated to spiritual discovery," I found myself muttering over and over. "If I'm not able to keep deepening within my marriage, why am I in it?"

Though it never got physical with Corena, I knew I'd have to tell Yvonne about her. That was a hell of a painful night.

Doug happened to be in town that evening, so he put on his facilitator's hat and listened to us talk about what wasn't working in our marriage.

She asked me the where's and when's with Corena.

I told her my three cylinder car image and asked her about her anger about the Forge. We were not getting very far.

Then I asked her,

"Remember when I told you about the openness I found at Mendham and with my Forge friends?" I knew this would be hard for her, but I had to go on. "It was really important to me. But when you got upset that it was with other people, not you, I just stopped telling you about what I was discovering. I cut it all off from you, even my excitements. But exploring this new way to be with people has been the most important thing in my life. I've been learning a ton but I can't share any of it with you."

"Yeah, and over the years you've tended to ridicule the things I've cared about," she responded, her voice as snappy and as angry as mine must have sounded. "I've stopped talking with you about some of the things that are important to me too."

Hearing this, I tried to apply what I'd been learning. I dropped down to feel her, belly to belly. In that space I said, deep and present, "I understand...I really do."

"And your interest in other people – Doug, Corena, your Forge friends – left me feeling cut out. I felt like I wasn't attractive."

Now centered even more deeply in my abdomen and hers, I nodded.

Just then Doug chimed in. "Can you feel the feelings she just shared with you? Of being rejected? Of being unattractive?"

"Of course," I told him, "I feel her right here, belly to belly," I said, motioning between both bellies. "Honest I'm feeling her right here." The Buddha himself would have been proud.

"That's nice," he said, unconvinced. "But honestly Bob, I can't feel you. She's telling you about where she hurts. And I'd have to say that frankly you look, well, kind of impassive.

"Let me ask you, have you ever felt rejected?"

"Oh sure," I answered, with energy.

"Well, how did that make you feel?"

"I hate it!" I said without thinking. "It was terrible when Carol rejected me and when Lisa pulled away. I hate it when Yvonne cocks her head back. I feel like I'm disappearing, like I don't exist. It's awful!"

"That's what she's probably feeling" Doug pointed out. "It's different than this quiet spiritual belly thing."

Long pause. This was registering.

"Is *that* what you're feeling," I asked her tentatively. "Do you feel like I've been rejecting you?"

"Yeah! Damn straight!"

"Oh..." Another pause. "Really?"

She nodded. I could see tears welling up.

"How awful!" I told her. "And are you feeling it even now?"

"Yessss," she said, in a hiss of anger and loneliness and betrayal and hurt.

"Oh, God" was the only thing I could say. "Have I been making you feel like *that*? Rejected? Disappeared, like I felt? I am *so* sorry!"

And the river blockage let loose a little. "How brutal I've been! I'm *so* sorry I've hurt you."

I really had been trying to tune into her. I really had been feeling her in my belly, centering into her with the kind of dropping down that had been so meaningful at Mendham. I really had been reaching for that trans-traditional spiritual connection, openness to openness. But I had missed who she was, her way. She didn't go into deep silence when she was feeling rejected. (Few of us do, frankly.) She felt hurt and angry, and that's a different place altogether.

She didn't need some abstract Buddha belly. She needed me to be with her, to feel her feelings, to know where I had hurt her. I'd been looking for that abstract, loving spiritual presence. And in the process I had missed *her*.

"Yeah, I feel totally cut out sometimes," she said, still angry. "And it hurts!"

Doug now turned to her. "Yvonne, he just acknowledged something that was hard for him. He just handed you a gift. That took a good bit of risk. But listening to you, it's as if nothing just happened. I don't see you acknowledging what he just offered you."

That seemed to register. She took a breath. And then she smiled, still clearly wary, and thanked me for acknowledging her pain.

As I had missed her in her terms, she had missed me in mine. "Yeah, it *was* a gift," she offered, a little more graciously now. "And yeah, I guess I missed you there. You *did* own up to some of your unconsciousness. I appreciate it. I really do."

And we had begun.

I'm pretty good at silence. I'm pretty good at opening inside or to trees or to ballet dancers. But to let go of my way of being spiritual, to open to her in her very different, very female, way called for a whole new way to be present. She was calling me to feel her loneliness—to which I myself had contributed.

I had to stop listening inside for my own spaciousness, step outside my own spiritual frame, and shift over to her way of being and feeling. I had to empathize in ways I wasn't used to. And frankly I wasn't particularly good at.

It was humbling as hell. Still is. I had to own up to my own defensiveness and the role my own spiritual commitments had played in keeping her at bay. I had to let go of my pretensions of being the poor but holy martyr. I had to own up that I, spiritual I, had helped create the distance between us. And she had to do something similar.

The very silence which had helped me emerge from a difficult youth, the open belly that had given me so much strength and on which I had based so much of my life, was now standing in the way of making contact with this woman I loved. My Buddha belly had become a Buddha wall.

Over the next few months piece after piece slowly drifted back into our marriage. Yes, she had resented my excitement about the Forge groups. Yes, I had snubbed her day care work. Yes we had stopped talking about her moral principles and about my writing. Yes she could be judgmental sometimes. Yes, so could I.

I had made her into a thing, an obstacle to be avoided or worked around, I told her, and she me. Gradually she was becoming a fully-fledged, real human being again. And someone I care deeply about.

Perhaps my divorced spiritual friends — Jane and Tom and Ethan — really did own up to how they themselves had helped shut out their spouses. Perhaps they were too ashamed to tell me. Maybe their partners really were as bad as they said. But my sense is that the fault has been at least partly theirs, not only their partners'. No one ever gets divorced because they themselves are part of the problem.

The freedom in a relationship, or lack of same, is always mutual, I suspect. I can't imagine someone closing off to mc if I wasn't at the same time shutting them out a little. Nor can I imagine making myself vulnerable too often if the other won't, at least a little, reciprocate. Only a masochist exposes their tender underbelly over and over if their partner doesn't, in rough parity, return the favor. Had Yvonne closed down or denied that she had missed me, I would have soon stopped. Had I begrudged her response, and raised my hand up against her again, she too would have closed down.

My sense though is that most people are indeed willing to tell real truth if it's safe enough, i.e. mutual enough. Generally, risk begets risk.

That evening, now eight years ago, was the beginning of my — our — education in building effortlessness into a long term relationship. I must say, opening to this woman since then, with whom I've cooked, laughed, raised kids, argued and had sex, this woman who just will not play by my rules, has been one of the most ego-challenging elements of my spiritual path. I've been meditating for four decades and carried silence for three and a half. Yet I had closed her out. Not intentionally, but I did, and I sometimes still do. I hurt someone I care about deeply. I am ashamed even now.

To love another human being, to be free long term with them, calls us to own up to the effects of our choices — beyond our own point of view. She has invited me outside the safety of my own conclusions and brings me face to face with the unintended consequences of my spiritual commitments. The very search for enlightenment to which I have dedicated my life, noble though it may be, has created distance from her and from others. Even my longings for a spiritual relationship probably got in the way, and may have hurt both of us. Long term openness calls us to look beyond the limits of what we believe.

Love, long term, real and open, is as damnable as it is wonderful. To acknowledge real truth about who I have and haven't been, to face my own contributions to another's pain, to own the disowned, is downright sobering. But even a relationship deeply scarred by our own neurotic limitations can become a home of grace.

God knows they discovered a lot. But it is here, in going solo, that Ramana Maharshi, St. Theresa and Rabia al-Adawiyya[100] gave up an enormous spiritual opportunity. Real intimacy offers up a spiritual challenge of the first order. It brings us nose to glass against the difference between our theory and real life, between universal love and the love of a real human being. To be with a soul who is unlike us can show us how our very aspirations, life commitments and certainties can not only save but entrap us. Long term intimacy teaches that spiritual progress, even the unmingling of consciousness from its content, can be defense as well as salvation.

It is this damnable and humbling gift that the celibate monk forsakes with his solitude. Did Ramana's silence cut him off, as it did me, even *as* it opened him up? Did Rabi'a too find it hard to acknowledge the distance she and her marvelous settledness may have created? The married life is not everyone's path, but for those of us who dare to undertake it seriously, a thoughtful, independent partner can call us at a level of honesty beyond any other I know, beyond all our elegant theories. No matter how wise we become, to love someone who refuses to be taken in by the hype of our own self talk is to be challenged, and then be challenged some more. Intimacy is a profound gift towards spiritual freedom.

And the sex is better.

Speaking of sex, I wonder how many of our “celibate” gurus, ministers, roshis or priests would be driven to promiscuity or pedophilia if they had put themselves in the salvific cauldron of long term intimacy? Would they have remained quite so unconscious of the effects of their actions?

Letting Go of the "But…"

Despite that breakthrough evening with Doug, over the next few years Yvonne and I managed to keep tangling an awful lot: arguments about child rearing, about car cleaning and about how to make pancakes. During one of them, piqued with anger, she tossed a zinger at me: "whenever you talk about our relationship there's always a 'but' in it. You'll say, 'We're becoming more open together," and then you'll add a 'but…' "Or you'll tell me you love me 'but…'

Just once I'd like to hear you say something about me or our marriage without a but."

I denied it of course. But the truth was, she was right. I *did* tend to name what she was *but* add what she wasn't. I *did* say where our marriage was good *but* also where it was flawed.

Later that night I decided to play a game with myself. Just to see what would happen, I would pretend for one year that there was no "but" in our relationship. Whenever I talked or thought about her or us, I vowed to myself, I'd make believe that our relationship was an "enlightened relationship," and that she had no flaws. I would re-evaluate my game the next January first.

Over the first few days of playing this game with myself, I did indeed catch myself thinking, "this is ok, but..." "she's cool but…" And every time I did, I told myself, "Nuh uh. You're not going there. No buts." And I would break the thought chain.

Within three weeks, oddly enough, something had shifted. I had stopped wondering whether the relationship was "enlightened" enough or if she was "open" enough. I had stopped comparing our marriage to *anything* else.

The marriage didn't suddenly become some la-la fantasy. Nor did it seem particularly awful. In fact emotionally it felt somewhat neutral. We just were what we were.

It is easy to understand why I kept adding that but, why I was so invested in my fantasies for our marriage. After all I'd found those amazingly open moments at Mendham and San Antonio. I'd learned a whole new way to be with some of my Forge friends. I'd even written about and run workshops on effortless or "sacred" relationships, for God's sake! (I'm writing about them here!) These are just the kind of relationships, I believed, that mirror and expand on enlightenment. No wonder I so wanted my marriage to live up to my picture!

But once again, I had to admit, I myself was a good bit of the problem. In holding out for "the enlightened partner," in clinging to my picture of "the sacred relationship", my own aspirations were blocking the very flow I was after. These were *my* pictures, *my* longings, not hers. And certainly not *ours.*

When I stop asking the questions—is this good enough? enlightened enough? – then all I have is wanting what is. As Jack Kornfield put this,

> *to want what you have and to not want what you don't have is the beginning of wisdom.*[101]

Only when I abandoned the search for the "infinite flow in relationship" could I find the flow in *this* one.

I wonder how many divorces have to do with some such longings—for the more perfect, sexier, more empathetic partner? I wonder how many divorces come from our own fantasies—how it's all supposed to be, feel, look, or make us feel? I wonder how many of us run away from our own buts?

The secret to bringing the freedom of the infinite into a long term relationship is, I think, to accept that every marriage is, in some sense, a disappointment.[102] And then face that.

> *The monk Ryokan said, "when you have a problem, face it; when you are sick, face it; when death stalks you, face it." To Ryokan it seemed obvious that when we face our difficulties we realize for the first time the shallowness of our complaints. Inner peace*

results from accepting one's limits and finding satisfaction within the incomplete.[103]

There are limits to how much disappointment we should bear, of course. If your partner beats you, that's clearly more disappointment than is good for you. If your partner is over-the-top verbally abusive or really, really, can't connect, well, maybe that too is more disappointment than is healthy. We all need to respect our limits.

But despite what we like to tell ourselves after the divorce, most people, even most ex's, are not sociopaths! Most are reasonably decent partner material.

In the end, what more can we ask for than decent partner material? Yvonne is actually *damn* decent partner material, now that I think about it. She and we have created a welcoming house. We have a sweet way of cuddling on the couch and we have a few dear friends. We have two fine and productive kids who occasionally call us to think out a problem or to celebrate a victory. I am satisfied with her indeed.

And I am dissatisfied with this woman. She can be stubborn and stuck and obsessive and she doesn't generally like to dialogue in the ways that I have found to work well. And I must admit I still don't clean the counters in the way she likes, nor hold up my end sometimes. Neither of us fulfills the other's fantasies.

Yet without the but, both disappointed and satisfied, I have been discovering the very relationship I was looking for! There is an ease to a non-judged marriage I did not expect. There is a readiness to flow into laughter or boredom or satisfaction or disappointment and even occasionally into magic. It's not like a wondrously peak meditation moment. It's rarely a moment of mutual mysticism. But we live and grow in intimacy every day, much as the silence grows quietly day after day.

The flow here involves moods, hers and mine. When holidays come and the children show up, she can get busy with cookies and wrapping, and we sometimes lose each other. When I get preoccupied with writing or worrying, I pull into my tortoise shell. My coming here to sink into the peculiar mystery of my life was a pulling away, and despite the nightly calls, we'll have to repair the distance I have unintentionally created. We will have to re-invent the openness with each other again, and it's always harder to recover than to lose. But at least it's no longer mine to do alone.

Love, real and long term, comes at you sideways. It comes in counting on someone to buy groceries or botch a good joke or just to be there year after year in all their obnoxiously unknowable Otherness, the ancient floodgates of wariness and distance worn through without noticing in a connection that is damn near unbearable.

To live and struggle with another human being for decades is to engage another's soul without resisting, and to grow towards a freedom I could not otherwise imagine. In its quiet profundity I am overwhelmed sometimes with feelings of "being with" so intense that I cannot speak without weeping.

If I tell the real truth, I was holding out for the perfect, neon light, "joy, eternal joy" relationship in part because I am afraid. Once I drop the fantasy, once I let down the crumbly old walls behind which I have been hiding my whole life, I come face to face with the inescapable fact that I will die first or she will, I will become disabled or demented first, or she will. I will lose her. And I do not know how I will bear it. The more you love, the more you become vulnerable. And I am afraid

No, I am not truly effortless yet in the face of real love. I don't know if I ever will be.

What calls me here is again the vastness. It's the same vastness that flowed into those tiny tubes in the back of my skull, grew in my life and wafted between mountains in the great cloud of unknowing. It's the same stuff.

What calls here, as there, is the same effortlessness, silent and real. Of this I am sure. This one is *in* the world, lived between more than felt, but it's the same stuff. It calls us to be here without holding back, to live its terrifying grace in the messiness of everyday connectedness.

"Do not settle," it whispers always. "Do not be content with partial love. Be open here too. Be so open with this other that there is nothing left to close."

Freedom beckons and beckons again. In relationship it calls us beyond our fantasies or of the perfect partner. "This may not be what you fantasized," it whispers. "This may not be not what you dreamed of. But she is a good soul, as are you. However humble and imperfect, be open, be truthful, together."

Learning to live jazz in the soul at this level of vulnerability has *got* to be part of today's spiritual goal.

If we cannot learn to live it, out loud, day after day, with another, if we cannot bring grace into our everyday, flawed, stinky old mutuality, it is not yet complete enough.

Walking with It

I wept when I wrote those last paragraphs. Sometimes the depth of all this is more than I can handle.

So after writing it I took a walk. Well, the dogs and I took a walk. Patch and Lil' Girl, the indefatigable pups from down the way, have been coming with me on my walks recently. I've been glad for their company.

For some reason tonight's evening air struck me as particularly sharp. The snow was almost crystalline in the cold, the light bright and vivid. The ice boughs overhead shimmered in the dusk like starlight chandeliers.

Off the lowest field, the three of us stumbled onto a new path that led mysteriously into the darkening woods. I had no idea where it was heading. If I tell the truth, I was a little afraid ... of getting lost perhaps? Or of some unexpected forest beast? (There *are* bears around, I've heard.) Yet, even so, there was a magic in walking into the unknown. The only sound was the snap of boots and paws breaking through frozen sheen. Even the dogs went quiet.

Yvonne and I had a few moments like this a couple of weeks ago. We were on a long drive and she was wondering aloud what she might want to do if she quits her job. I can probably count on one hand the times that this competent woman really didn't know where she was going. We were both, I think, a little afraid. And enchanted. I wanted to hold my breath.

We didn't come up with an answer that day. I didn't actually care. What I liked was being with her in *not* knowing.

I think this is part of what I loved at Mendham and with Doug: being with others where we do not yet know. I treasured my hours with Corena in part because we were so *not* in charge. I tried not to breathe those moments with Yvonne because they were so mysterious, so alive.

Eventually the dogs and I found our way through the frozen marsh into an unnoticed corner of a cornfield. We were just below my hermitage, back to the everyday. So too Yvonne and I soon found our way back to the already-known.

I'd like to live in the unknowing more. But maybe this is just the deal: even undergirded by stillness, you only get a few minutes of mystery. And then you're back again to old cornfields and hay mows.

Mystery comes, almost always, in brief flashes. But it's out there, and it keeps beckoning. We stumble unexpectedly into the magic, we take one more step into what we don't yet know. And then we pull back. Sometimes we forget what we discovered, sometimes it becomes the new ordinary.

And then after awhile, we stumble again into the not-yet-known, and feel our way to the next new norm. The magic is brief but never quite forgotten. It quiets down, but it never quite lets up, or at least I hope not. Newness, order, chaos, then new order again. Repeat.

It was good to have Patch and Lil Girl with me tonight. And it was good to be with Yvonne that afternoon in the car. Being with fellow pilgrims seems to help somehow. Holding another's hand in the face of the tsunami of what cannot be known is one of the kinder gifts that come with being human.

Chapter 8

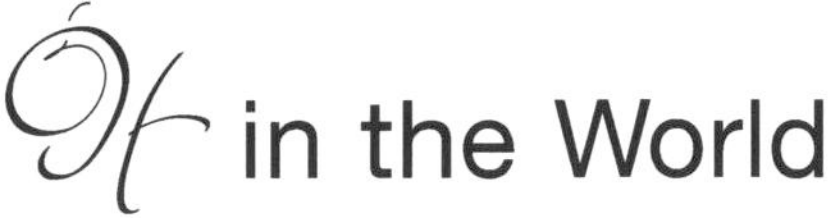

Unresistant to It

My life has been punctuated with meditation retreats. Maharishi used to describe meditative growth as like dipping a cloth into the dye, then exposing it to the sun, thus slowly making the color fast. I'm not sure if the dyeing happens between my retreats or during, but some of the color does seem to have gotten a little faster over the years.

In 1997, some three years after that drive from Crestone down to Denver, I took a retreat in the deciduously forested Lynwood Retreat Center in upstate New York. After two days of catching up on sleep, always needed, I began to feel this strangely insistent sensation that I was as if a pyramid or mountain; my crossed legs were its base and my head its summit.

I don't usually get images in meditation, certainly not in one meditation after another like that. But this odd sensation was growing more insistent day by day. It was like being the pyramid on the back of the dollar bill.

After several days I began to feel an intense energy focusing in my forehead, as if a dozen spotlights were aiming from within at my "third eye." And after a few more days, these sensations suddenly disappeared.

My attention now shifted higher up, to just *above* my head. I could feel something like a yellow or gold Mohawk up there, more like a sensation of light or energy than of hair. Actually I'm not sure I should call it a sensation. Though it was as much a part of me as is my left hand, it was *above* my skull, *beyond* the limits of my skin.

This Mohawk thing also lasted for several days. I went over what little I knew about the sixth and seventh chakras, which according to Hinduism are respectively in the forehead and atop the head. What I had been feeling was similar, but in neither case were these "sensations" what I might have expected.

The 6th chakra is said to be mid-forehead, radiating outwards from the third eye. But here the radiation was coming from within, and pointing *inside* my skull. And what was this weird mountain sensation?

The crown or 7th chakra sits atop the skull. But it is generally pictured as a lotus, which is bowl shaped. This long, narrow Mohawk sensation didn't quite fit. (Perhaps traditional depictions are more like generic portraits, and different physiologies might give rise to different particulars.) Whatever this was, it was quite mythic.

All very beseeching. But what really got me was the drive home. I took the scenic route down the Taconic. I'd been driving perhaps half an hour when once again something seemed weird in how I was seeing. I'd gotten used to these drives by then, so I pulled the car over to get a fix on it, leaving the radio on and the engine rumbling idly.

In front of me was a small, nearly square reflective green sign, bolted neatly atop its three foot pole with 45/7 printed on it in reflective Helvetica. A mile marker, I figured, 45.7 miles from wherever the Taconic begins.

As I looked at it, something seemed odd. Whatever this strange sense was, it wasn't like that cloud in Colorado ... No, not in my peripheral vision, I thought ... No, this one has something to do with how I am looking ... something is weird about how I am seeing this mile marker …

And suddenly I knew. For the first time in my life, I *was* what I was seeing. I *was* that mile marker.

Every "it" I'd ever looked at had always been "over there." I had been "over here." Whatever I saw, tasted or touched always had been, as the existentialist philosophers describe it, "over-against" me. Always that existential split — I/you, me/it — and a felt wall in between. Every single thing I had ever encountered had been "other."

But not that unassuming little mile marker. There was no boundary between me and it, no "over against," no "other."

Or to describe it from the other side, I was not pulling away inside, even a smidgeon, from it. Nor, as I looked around, was I pulling away from the forest … or from the stream below the road … or from the bluegrass on the radio. Nothing was other. I couldn't sense any separation anywhere.

I noticed a Yellow Shafted Flicker clinging to an oak tree behind the little sign. I watched him beat-beat-glide his way down to the ground and start pecking. I wasn't *resisting* him in the way I always had. Even though he was a different being, I wasn't afraid of him even subtly, as I would have been. Nothing inside was pulling away. Though I could still judge feet and inches — he was about 20 feet away — there was no felt distance from him. It was as if my skin had become porous.[104]

I flashed back to that experience of the cloud in the Colorado valleys. In comparison, this being with the Flicker and the mile marker seemed … well … *ordinary.* No great expanse, no exciting interpenetration. No photogenic cloud. This seemed rather plain, actually, down to earth. I just wasn't pulling back. I was just being with.

Perhaps this very ordinariness is part of why this new relationship, or non-relationship, has remained with me ever since. Never again have I experienced that old feeling of distance or that sense of "otherness" towards things. If anything, the non-resistance to the external world has only become more obvious.

Now don't get me wrong. I didn't used to be any more antagonistic to the world or other people than the next fellow. We probably all pull back just the teeniest bit from the world—with the slightest hint of defense or protection. I believe that how I used to be in the world is pretty standard.

It's quite necessary. We need to build boundaries, God knows. Even as tiny babies we have to construct our sense of a separate self. We need to know where we stop and our mom or the crib begins.

Without learning these simple lessons we could never build a sense of an I, never learn that we are separate from our parents or other kids, never know ourselves to be autonomous. And God forbid that we should not create boundaries with a smothering mother or some abusive boyfriend! No, it's very important to have edges.

But if you're reading this book, you've probably learned this lesson pretty well. You probably know by now where you end and the world begins. (Except, of course, for the inevitable boundary confusions we all have with our spouses!)

I created my borders, I could see as I compared it with this new sense, with a subtle kind of internal pushing away. It's like inside I held up my hand, just a little, with a felt-sense of "stop right there, buster!" I never realized that I was doing it, of course. I can't imagine how I could have. But I was resisting ever so slightly inside. And towards absolutely everything. I was, "Come thou no closer."

I had been holding every bird, every glass of water and every waving branch with the same kind of psychic distancing as I did the most intrusive parent or dangerous thug.

But over against that Yellow Shafted Flicker, over against that mile marker, there was no upraised hand, not even a finger.

We probably don't need to work so hard all the time to maintain our boundaries like we do. That Flicker was awfully small; it really wasn't much of a danger to me. And mile markers truly are harmless. Really, we don't need to protect ourselves against every bird, every mile marker and every piece of music, do we?

Since that day, resisting far less, it's become a little easier just to be. At some deep existential level I'm no longer holding things at bay. Birds, cranberry bread, everyone I meet, even the wind—the world just has fewer boundaries now.

Perhaps this is why just now I can feel the breeze in my chest so clearly and the snowy maple branches across the back of my shoulders. For I am *in* the trees outside the window in a way I couldn't have imagined, and the woods have found their way into my little hermitage.

Success and Failure in It

I think we all have one or two core life problems: being seen, gaining love, finding a life passion or focus in an over-busy life, gaining respect. Mine is neatly put in a line from the Gita:

> *Do the duty (dharma) to which you are called, oh Arjuna,*
> *Indifferent to success and failure.*[105]

Becoming "indifferent to success and failure" isn't everyone's core problem, but it's been one of mine. (At this stage, it's pretty clear that there's little relationship between spiritual and material success. But hey, you have to learn this somehow.)

In the upper middle class Jewish suburb in which I came of age, I heard endless paeans of success: "he's a successful Doctor now," "... he graduated *summa* from law school and now..." "made a fortune in real estate." To be a success was to be worthwhile. My folks, my friends, my teachers and above all I bought the narrative. "Successful" "wealthy," "famous" was roughly equivalent to "yeah! good guy!" It was never "be the best you can be" or "be the authentic you," or "love and be loved." Just "be the best," "be a success," "earn a lot." You know, "the guy with the biggest bankbook when he dies wins."

So when, in late 2004, The Forge Institute that I had founded was losing members, people were bellyaching and many of our volunteers had lost their enthusiasm, I was staring — embarrassed, scared and ashamed — into the maw.

I made excuses, of course. "Not my fault." "We're ahead of our times." "Got bad advice." "Underfunded."

All true. And all irrelevant. All I knew was I was falling apart.

So one September afternoon I said to myself "I've got to get a handle on this!" and started walking, glum but determined, up the hill to nearby Draper Park. I found a peeling park bench as far from the people and dogs as I could, with a view of the Palisades and the expansive mouth of the Hudson River. I asked myself,

"Ok, what's going on here Bob?" Instantly, terror.

It took awhile to settle down. But I'd been here before. So I turned around inside and asked myself, "OK, kid. Just what's so scary about all this? Is there some truth you're not willing to tell yourself here?"

The answer was obvious. I just didn't want to say it. I was failing.

So I whispered it to myself, barely audible above the breeze: "What I don't want to say is, I am failing." My belly clenched. I wanted to run away. There was clearly gold here.

So I said it again, still half whispering: "I am failing." The very words I least wanted to say.

"I am failing," I said, again, still afraid.

Honestly to say this aloud felt like breaking some sort of law. I cannot fail. We must not fail. And if we do, we are never to acknowledge it. Failure is forbidden.

So I said it again, "I am failing."

I could see my mother in the dining room, turning away. I saw my father at his desk, waving me away with a mere puff and a wave of the hand. In each image I was left alone, ignored, falling, in some sort of chasm.

I stayed on that bench for nearly an hour, failing.

Over the next few afternoons I wandered up to that park bench. I'd feel the breeze. I'd look out over the expansive Hudson. I'd recite my new mantra—"I am failing." And I'd feel like crying.

Looking out over that wide, wide river, I began to feel as if I was on it, floating face up in its great grey characterless breadth. Some ancient dread was here: of being a tiny bauble, afloat, nowhere in particular, lost utterly. I was a speck in an enormous ocean, alone.

"I am failing…I am failing"

To fail in our culture is to disappear, to be nothing in a sea of nothing, to fade away, utterly and without a trace. As Clapton put it, "nobody knows you when you're down and out."[106] The failed do not exist. And they never did.

"I am failing, failing."

Facing abandonment for those weeks, floating meaninglessly in a grey and characterless sea was the loneliest experience I have ever had. No islands, no place to stand or to plant your flag. Just lost, directionless, disappeared, alone. Utterly alone.

I had been running from this sinking lostness all my life. It was behind my drive for A's in school, behind every seductive come-on, behind all that craving for the approval of Professor Brereton, Professor Proudfoot, and all of them. It was behind every anxious ambition, behind every drive for fame and every silly thing I said to get noticed. It was craving to *be,* a need to plant a flag in the placelessness at the core of my life. It was a craving to exist.

"I am failing."

This wasn't about what had actually happened in my life. I had not been a total failure; I knew that. I'd earned a Ph.D, published ten books, started a journal and a non profit, brought value into the world. Now, this wasn't about overt accomplishments. This was about what had been behind *all* those cravings: this existential fear, the terror of not existing. I was about one year old, perhaps, left outside crying too long, nobody noticing. It was about being left alone, forgotten, unseen. Whatever it was, this was deep and ancient and unquenchable.

Every afternoon for nearly two weeks I trudged up to that park. I'd sit on my peeling park bench, look out over the wide, wide Hudson, and fail. It was as painful and lonely and abandoned as anything I'd ever faced. Yet it felt somehow important. Alone, awake, I'd disappear into an endless sea of loneliness.

I had not been running from failure. I had been running from not existing.

After perhaps two and a half weeks, I walked up that hill, planted myself on my bench, looked out over the Hudson and said my mantra, "I am failing." And…nothing.

I said it louder, "I am failing." No sinking dread. No bitter taste.

I yelled it: "You're a god-damned failure!"

All I felt was a cool breeze coming up from the Hudson. I watched tiny ripples vee out from a tug slowly pulling a barge up the river. And I went home.

I don't know how we human beings can ever become complete without spreading our arms wide to the very pain from which we have run from all our lives.

That which haunts us will always find a way out.
That wound will not heal unless given witness.
The shadow that follows us in the way in.
Rumi

I know no better way to give such witness than to sit on a park bench, alone, patient, eyes wide open, staring into the maw of the very truth that most terrorizes us. It was only when I faced my dread of not existing without flinching that I came to see and to own my lifelong desperation. And not the other way around.

But the emotional neutrality I found is its own kind of gift. There is a peace in neutrality you don't expect. When you have stared straight into the frightening maw of your great fear, what you get is … well, life. You just go about living. There's an understated ease in such neutrality. It's not ecstasy, it's not bliss. Nor is it nothing.

About three months later, we held one of our bi-weekly Forge Hearths, our small group for mutual deepening. Only Persephone and DeAnne had come. "Two people," I thought to myself. "It's clearly too small. Why aren't they flocking to this in droves?"

But that habitual self-flagellation didn't really resonate. What I found myself noticing was that these two women were doing *such* good work.

"You know what I haven't been admitting to myself…?"

"I think what I've been withholding from Steven is …"

"You know, listening to you, I think I've been lying to David as well…"

It wasn't me, of course. These wonderful women were doing the letting go. But I was their facilitator, friend and mentor. And I was helping.

"This isn't flashy work," I said to myself. "It's not generating millions. I'm not getting famous. But I'm helping these two good people. And they're helping me too. It is good to be here tonight."

Becoming free of what has haunted you is a good thing. It's not good because you're succeeding or getting famous or answering your childhood longings. It's not good because Dad approves. It's just good to mature and transform and to grow in love and self-honesty.

Helping people find themselves or deepen with one another has always been the point of my work. But that was the first evening in which I was satisfied *only* because I was helping. And that sad old demon—the one that needed success or approval or to exist—just wasn't in the room that night.

Success is an if/then statement. *If* I become famous *then* people will really love me. *If* I get rich then I'll really be OK. And it's always about tomorrow: ah, *then* they'll really see me!

That evening though there was no tomorrow. There was only Persephone, DeAnne and me. There was nothing fancy to come. There was nothing scary to be afraid of. Just us, doing the work, quietly becoming more open, together.

Today, some five years later, writing these recollections in my little hermitage, I still watch myself flip occasionally into some future-fantasy. This book will be a hit; people will think I was heroic to come here, I'll be admired. Deep longings like these fade slowly.

But then I catch myself and I give a little chuckle, "Ha, there you go again!" And then I say, "nah, not today fellah. Come back, here, now." I didn't used to be able to do this.

I was half expecting that if you found your "appointed duty" or answered your cosmic *dharma*, then all those old cravings would suddenly vanish, as if you'd turned off a switch. Maharishi made it sound so easy.

Here I was pretty sure that I had indeed found my *dharma,* my real calling. But being able to do my appointed duty while "indifferent to success and failure" has come more slowly, more organically. I topple unexpectedly into some future fantasy. I catch myself. It happens again. I catch myself again. Sometimes I laugh at myself. And maybe, just maybe, I do so less and catch myself a tad quicker.

To learn how to be a human being enmeshed in permanent silence is, as the Nicene Creed has it, to learn how to be "fully God and fully man." It is to learn to be silent *and* noisy, wrestling with ancient demons *and* be spacious. It is to live in the soul, one foot in the great cosmic infinite and the other in the leftovers from imperfect parents, half-formed siblings and childish friends, not to mention our own troubled histories. And silence cures some of our dysfunctions, but only some. Curing a life, in my case becoming truly "indifferent to success and failure" (or whatever is our life issue) is where this all gets lived.

Just at this moment I'm feeling pretty free of the good or ill fantasy. I am without tomorrow or yesterday, without success, without failure. What I feel is actually quite simple, almost flat. I just make the toast or write these words or pad over to my meditation perch. There are no accolades here, no hopes, no longings. And no failing. It all feels so … so … *normal*!

Yawning the World into It

About two years later one last jigsaw piece clicked into place. Another ten day retreat, here in upstate NY, during a muggy late August, 2000. I noticed during one afternoon meditation that that my breathing had become, just for a few seconds, utterly effortless. All those tiny throat tightenings, the small catches in the breath that you barely notice, had suddenly disappeared. For four or maybe five breaths, my breathing machinery was utterly frictionless.

Again, you don't notice consistent patterns like these till they fade away. But up until those few seconds, every breath had been, ever so slightly, balky: a pause here, a catch there, something opening only halfway. It had all been very faint, barely noticed, but constant. Here though, for just a few seconds, it took no effort to breathe. None. Breathe in. Breathe out. It was that easy.

Over the next few days it happened a few more times. I'd notice that the muscles behind my ears would relax, my jaw would let down ever so slightly, and my whole breathing apparatus would again become smooth. I even took a few breaths that way during a walk. It felt quite sweet, actually. It was easier than usual just to be.

Breathing with no resistance whatsoever was remarkable, if something so normal can be said to be remarkable. It's as if nothing at all was stopping me from the inside and nothing from the outside. So I just breathed, with no hesitation whatsoever.

Breathing on a walk without a hair of resistance, came to feel that I was *inhaling* the trees, the hills, the stones on the driveway. I was as if I was sucking the trees and clouds sky deep into my lungs. I seemed to have become some great world devouring maw. I felt frankly like I was yawning in the world.

This yawning thing happened a few more times on that retreat.

Every time I went on retreat over the next few years, and for longer and longer periods, it would happen again. The muscles inside my ears would relax, the sides towards the back of my throat would open, and my breathing would become again utterly liquid. It stayed for longer periods on my walks or even sometimes in my hermitage. I seemed to be inhaling the world, more and more often, into some great emptiness. It's a strange feeling, yawning in trees, stones, seed pods, like you're huge and growing larger.

This happened only on meditation retreats for the next four or five years. Then one day, back in New York, walking by Madison Square Garden on 8th Ave, I realized that I was breathing that way again. The cracks on the sidewalk, the bodega's colorful fruit, the taxicabs speeding down 8th — I was inhaling them all in, like some great urban vacuum.

This strangely easy way of being has stayed with me most of the time since then. I don't think about my breathing much, but when I pay attention, it's still frictionless. Though it's less of a striking difference than some of the other shifts, I suppose I'd have to say this too has become permanent.

This, and the lack of separation from what I see, is I suspect, the real unity consciousness the mystics they talk about. It is deep and real. What I didn't expect is how ordinary it has come to seem.

It's quite different from what I expected and from how many spiritual teachers describe such mystical unity, or what Evelyn Underwood called "The Prayer of Union.[107]" It's *not* that I have no defensiveness. I like to think I'm less defensive than I used to be, but I still get emotionally defended sometimes, even while breathing in the world. If someone gets very aggressive with me or if I feel like I haven't been heard, my emotional machinery may still click into protective mode. Unity consciousness is, again, not a personality transplant.

The odd thing is that even when I get defensive, this sense of non resistant unity, this sense of breathing in the world or the other person, remains. It lives somehow *beneath* my feelings and my self-protective instincts. But it's there. I can be *emotionally* defensive yet existentially non-resistant. Not quite the "we are the world" that we expected, huh?

Now, would you allow me a moment to rant? (if not, skip this paragraph) Recently I heard some self help guru (who will remain nameless) encourage her audience to "try to experience the oneness of all things." I find that terribly misleading, even a little silly. To pretend that you feel connected may work for a few minutes, but it's a *thought* of connection, not an existential connection. The problem is not only that it's imagined, a chimera, but it may lead to denying real feelings of separation or real feelings. And it reveals a deep misunderstanding. Unity consciousness is *not* an emotion. It is *not* something we can think up or make ourselves feel. It is a real shift in the relationship between consciousness and its objects. Consciousness comes to perceive itself—without effort—as none other than its contents. It comes at a level beneath trying, beneath imagining, beneath even the idea of oneness. Such a change is deep, structural and important, not something we think or pretend or try to make happen. It may lead, indirectly, to some personality or attitude changes. But these are the *result* of the structural shift, not the other way round. Please, let's not imitate or pretend some mood of oneness, but rather work to shift ourselves into the real thing.

Ok, thanks. I'm done now.

Now, back to it. It's now been five years since that breathing shift. It's rare to feel one of those breath-shudders or throat-catches that used to be so common. Nor have I felt that muscle behind my ears let go for a long time now. I've lost the surprising feeling of yawning the world in, which probably had to do with the newness of this sort of breathing. The unity with what I see and the non-resistant breathing has become second nature, I suppose. So that just now the trees, the snow sparkling outside my window and the stove rumbling alongside me are all somehow welcome inside me, in my body, in my lungs, far more viscerally and comfortably than was even that road sign or Flicker. My breathing, the world and the shimmering snow now seem like some vast connective tissue. The snow showering off the branches and glittering on the pods are here, inside the hermitage, deep inside my pectoral muscles.

It's hard to remember how hard the world used to be. But I'm sure it's easier now. The world has become kindly, as if I'm being held. Even the plaster walls across the room seem softer somehow. The room, the wind and the snowy pods outside have become buttery.

Maybe this is just the mellowing of age. Maybe everyone feels similarly by 60. Perhaps all the meditation and therapy and reflection these past 40 years have just helped me relinquish the worst of the fears and terrors with which I came of age. Or maybe I started out with more of a deficit than most, and all I've done is to take a particularly long route to "normal."

But I doubt it. Somehow knowing the trees in my belly and experiencing the softness of plaster walls seems like an unusually generous gift. Maybe this is what is given to people who spend their lives relinquishing the fears and the smallnesses of their youth enough to see, just a little more clearly, how things actually are.

Years of meditation and self reflection and retreats don't make us rich and they don't make us famous. But they may help us face the illusions of our ancient terrors. And when we do, when we can finally drop those hands that we've been holding up against the world, when we are finally able to relax into the simple presence of being from which we have been running all our lives, what seems to come is a world that feels like a kiss.

This too seems to be a piece, and an important one, of today's complete spiritual goal. To live in a world that is no longer so over-against us, no longer so threatening, to experience the deep and unspeakable connection that lives below our thoughts and our feelings, is I think, to live closer to what is deeply so.

Chapter 9

Working in It

A Team in It

I've come to love it here, the fire warm on my shoulder, the gentle sway of my chair, the chimney's crackling with the first heat. The cabin is deliciously quiet this morning. Solitude has been one of the surprising gifts of being here.

As I think about what I want to write this morning, I find myself going away from here, dropping in and down to listen for what wants to be said, then coming up and out with a breath, and back to here. It's a pendulum of attention: up to eyes and shoulders, then down and inside, down and to the page. Then another breath, up and out to walls and warmth, then dropping again, and all on the quiet presence of the vast.

What is beneath does not swing with my swings, though it's my sense that it makes it easier to notice. It just is. I am not *trying* to "be here now." Trying to remember consciousness or solitude when I'm pondering something else would be a distraction, as I see it, not a spiritual act. Of *course* I won't be paying attention to being awake or to the crinkling of the chimney when I'm remembering a past experience or trying to articulate a point! I think one of the gifts I've received from meditation was that I *don't* have to remind myself to notice awakeness or unity with the walls. The effortlessness of all this is part of it, as is the natural flow of the trend line.

Which leads me to what I want to explore today. The shifts I had been witnessing were mostly changes in how *I* hold *myself*, another or the world. Until the discoveries with Corena, Doug and Yvonne, they were all encountered by or in *me*.

But something else had been calling me ever since that group mysticism at Mendham. At this point I'd call it a new *domain* for awakening. I came back from my meditation retreats and even did some good work on my psychologist's couch, but I still struggled with departmental politics at the colleges I taught in. Others get bollixed up by the politics in their offices or baseball teams or some village board's dysfunctions. We can free up a lot from our side to help us avoid being toppled by these. Nonetheless, there's a crabbed quality in the thinking, working and creativity of such ill-functioning groups. It cannot but effect our life and work.

If freedom is to be complete it can and must open up to what is beyond me: to the communities and organizations I inhabit. Enlightenment Plus will have to be big enough to foster soul jazz in our teams, communicates, church boards and other groups.

And it turns out that this domain of awakening has enormous, unexpected benefits.

The Forge Institute had created a Guild for spiritual teachers, founded local communities, built college programs. But by 2005 none of it seemed to be working. We on the board had lots of theories why membership and income were declining. But the real problem, I'd say now, was that we had not yet figured out how to help people reliably enter and stay in the mutual vastness. We didn't have a teaching. But I get ahead of myself.

The eight of us on the board rented a cabin in the mountains of North Carolina for a five day "Vision Quest for The Forge." We started with 24 hours of silent meditation. Then we told each other what we sensed was being called for from us: "soul to soul contact," the "joy of playing at the depths alone and together," "finding the freedom of the real."

We thought about how to help folks do these things better. We offered theories. We drew charts. But the magic wasn't happening in our midst and at some level we all knew it.

On day three, after one of his particularly colorful diagrams was shot down, Michael, our newest board member, blurted out,

"Hey! Come on!" His voice was tight and loud. "I don't feel like you're really listening! This is a damn good idea! But it doesn't seem to be registering. This is my third or even fourth proposal. But unless you three guys from the early board think up an idea, I'd swear it doesn't get heard.

"I feel like I'm hitting my head against a wall." Angrier now, "you three hang together like some sort of impenetrable inner circle. I'm really fed up!"

Mary Ellen chimed in. "You know, Michael, I'd have to say that sometimes I feel the same way. It's like unless Bob, Doug or Phil go for an idea, it just fades away. Sometimes it *is* hard to break in."

"But," I stammered defensively, "we're the ones who do the work. If you want to get something heard, just make it happen. I know I for one will listen!"

"I'll be happy to make them happen, honest!" Michael went on, louder now. "But I've *already* put out some damn good ideas. And I'm sure as hell not going to work on them if nobody listens! It's like you three fend me off with some quippy remark or laughter, but don't really take me seriously. It's like there's this inner circle at the core of the board, and the rest of us don't really count. How can someone one break in around here?"

This was hard to hear. But it had the unmistakable thud of truth.

Phil spoke up first. He turned thoughtfully to Doug and me, "You know, maybe Michael's got a point. The three of us have been in this for years, God knows, and we like to play around together. I could see how our little cabal might seem pretty hard to crack into.

"And we'll have to admit," he went on, "this is not the first time we've heard something like this. Remember when Peter and Kay said they both felt a little on the margins?"

Another long pause.

"Maybe..." I began hesitantly. "Maybe the three of us *have* been playing things pretty close to the chest. Maybe our kidding around with each other has been a subtle way to keep the real cards to ourselves, fending others off a little. I bet I'd be a little pissed off too if my suggestions weren't registering. Yeah, I can see it *would* be hard to break in."

"Yeah," Michael concurred, softening a little. "It's like nobody can break in here."

"It's what I said, like you guys don't really hear me," added Mary Ellen, tearing up. "It's like you don't care what I think."

"I know," Phil went on, "we've not done it on purpose. But I can see how we've not listened to Michael very well. He *has* made some damn good suggestions. I can see how we might look a little like an old guard around here. How embarrassing is this?"

Doug then turned to Michael, Mary Ellen and the others : "Does this sound right? Do you guys feel like the three of us have been using our friendship to hang onto some of the power here?"

Nods. Smiles. Kindly eyebrows.

"Well, I'll be damned!" said Doug, clearly moved. "I had no idea!"

Smiling a little more, Michael was visibly touched. "I'm sooooo glad to hear you guys talking like this. I doubt it's been conscious on your part. But yeah, there *is* a power core around here, a circle within the circle. It *has* been hard to get heard."

"This feels really important to me too," said Tom Feldman, our board chair, continuing in his softening tone. "You guys do seem willing to face your own stuff here. I'd say there's a little more space in the room."

"I think I'm starting to get this," I told them. "It's like my quickness and friendship with Doug and Phil was some odd kind of self protection. I've been using my kidding around as some kind of control thing. It sure wasn't on purpose, but when I look at how you must have felt …

"I want to say this clean" I said, looking around the now silent room. "I have done this to you. Again, I wasn't aware I was doing this. But I *have* been cutting you guys out. …

These were my friends and people I truly respected and I, we three, had been doing with. It was registering. "I am," now with a catch in my throat, "truly sorry."

It was obvious. Phil and Doug saw it too, and both acknowledged that they'd played their role as well.

Smiles. Nods. Contact. Coos.

We talked about how we'd each felt. We named what had been going on in the little core group, and how it felt to be excluded, and who did what when. Eventually everyone in the room felt their way into something of their own roles in the pattern. We teased out some of our ambivalence about control.

More smiles, nods and contact.

Then we got to talking about the process we had just gone through together, the blocks and breakthroughs, and the sense of spaciousness that was now in the room. How different this was from the kind of opening than we'd found in our meditation halls and how the same. And how sweet it was to find it here together.

"You know," Michael said thoughtfully, "what I was trying to say before all this was that I bet we could cook up one hellova program to *teach* the sort of thing we've just gone through. We broke through something inside ourselves but also with each other. Together we found something freer, the spacious, the non-dual. I've been in the self-help, spiritual teaching world a long time and I know this is something new. There's an unleashing here that most people don't know how to do. Why can't we teach *this*?

"Yeah, why not?" Phil agreed, clearly intrigued.

Tom said, "Seems to me the key was that we didn't run from our tension. We felt the scariness, felt the anxiety, and used it as our gateway to opening the space. Why can't we teach *that?"*

"Yeah," added Melissa, with growing excitement. "We *used* our tensions here, we didn't run from them. Why couldn't we teach people to do *that*?"

"There has been some truly co-creative energy here," added Doug. "We've got *lots* of tools in our toolbox that can help here."

Kerry Gordon jumped in: "How about teaching people how to confront the anxieties that come up not just in conflict but *any* time we face into something new?"

"Yeah," me now, "The freedom we're seeing in a group is the

same freedom we can find alone. This is *not* only about communication or group work. It's about finding the sacred inside *or* out."

"I like this a lot," Melissa this time, "teaching people to be as free in groups as well as we can get alone."

"Yeah, both," added Mary Ellen. "But as we teach this stuff, let's make sure we don't lose the kind of tone we've been finding even while we're teaching it."

"Yeah," Phil now, "whatever we teach, let's give people the direct experience of interacting at this level of honesty and freedom, maybe like a workshop."

Mary Ellen again, "I think there's been something of the masculine / feminine energies in our tensions. Everybody has to deal with these. Maybe there could be something in a workshop around the boy/girl thing too."

"If we did a workshop," Michael added, "we'd have to do something on the web. You can't just offer face to face any more. We'll have to have both."

"Yeah," Kerry added, "both. There must be lots of ways to help people create this jazz in the soul."

"Hey, there's our name for it," I tossed out. "Let's call it Soul Jazz!"

That one got oohs.

"Well how much would we have to charge to make something like this pay for itself…?"

"What kind of web site would we need to offer both …?"

It actually was like jazz, those two days. Doug invites Michael to flesh out an idea, Mary Ellen finds a gem in the confusion and adds her own thoughts. I key off Melissa's concerns, Phil's riffs off Tom and Kerry. We formed teams. We modeled. We drew charts. We roughed out financials. It was trust and humor and surprise and listening and damn good jammin'. The dance floor was open and we were boogieing.

We've found this sort of co-creative space, more or less, as we've continued to develop and test these programs in months and months of conference calls and meetings since those days. As of today, I don't know if what we've cooked up—the Soul Jazz webinars and workshops—will work well enough. I'll tell you in a few years. But we have been creating and then re-creating the very freewheeling group energy that we teach, and doing some excellent work!

The difference between this and most other groups I've been in, including the disappointment at New Orleans, was that with this gang when tensions come up, we're each willing to speak honest, self-critical truth. Doug and Phil and I and eventually everyone has pretty much owned up to our dark sides, out loud. We've lost and rebuilt, lost and rebuilt, the trust and heart to heart connection it takes to create together.

At this point I'd say that the tensions that are often stumbling blocks arc usually our way in. The blockages often hide our differences and confusions and once there are no more secret patterns to be denied or hurt feelings to be ducked, we can get creative about whatever problem we're dealing with with fairly unabashed creativity. It's like you go from being crouched over in protection to being able to stand up straight and just play.

I was smarter and more creative than I generally am during those days. I'm smarter on our conference calls than I am alone. I know we all feel this way.

When the secrets are out and everyone's defenses are down, I'd swear we can enter something like a group consciousness. Whatever it is, it is a free flowing group brilliance, a mutual jazz in the soul riffing. And you just don't know it's possible until you're part of it.

This mutual consciousness-lifting, this co creative spaciousness is the domain of awakening I mentioned at the outset. One person's thoughts stimulate another's, and theirs a third and forth. It's awakening a collective consciousness.

You can be fully awake, even non dual, and still not know this level of awakening.

I want more of this. I do not want to be bound by the limitations of my own mind. I want to be smarter and I want to have this kind of fun with others who can sustain this kind of flow with me. I want to speak and jam and play and work with others only in this kind of co-creative mutuality. It's just not much fun to be on teams that are politicized or in communities that are grumpy, and the work isn't nearly as inventive. I want to be with others who all stand up straight and jam with abandon. It is, as I said, a whole new domain for awakening. And I like it.

I don't have enough experience to say if any organization today can remain truly unresistant for long. But it is possible—I know it—and if it isn't yet, it certainly should be!

It will take profoundly flexible managers and employees and ongoing discipline to keep an organization's relationships clean and above board. It will take leaders who can listen especially non-defensively for better ideas than their own, and the flexibility of everyone involved to be deeply honest about others and mostly themselves. It will require clear and inspiring missions, for a magnetic purpose is to an organization what the transcendent is to an individual.

Why can't we give life and voice to such mutual and creative freedom in our organizations, schools and corporations? Why can't our baseball teams, school and church communities and even, perhaps, our politics (though that one is hard to imagine, given what we see today) awaken.

This would be part of a life of freedom all the way down.

Effortless openness in a co-creative group is of a piece with the openness we've discovered at the feet of our gurus or ministers. The tools are different though. The rules of interpersonal engagement are parallel to but different than the rules of meditation, prayer or even psychological growth. They involve the arts of listening, of truth telling, of learning how to break through your own power issues.

But they are both gifts of grace.

Silence at Work, Writ Large

One more jigsaw piece. (I'd like to say "one final piece" but this is a work in progress and I don't know if we ever get to the end.)

About a year after that board meeting, I was invited to speak to a gathering of "Humanity's Team," a spiritual/political outreach group founded by Neale Donald Walsh, at Bard College. I had prepared a pretty good talk, I thought. Had some pretty nifty powerpoint slides. But by the time I'd spent a day there and gotten to know the crowd of 200, it was obvious that what I had written was way off. They were far more homogeneous—more Catholic, middle class and enthusiastic—than I'd expected. And they seemed largely unaware of the enormous spiritual movement of which they were an obvious part. When my time came, I left my prepared notes on the chair and just started talking.

I spoke more from the heart than the head. I complimented their obvious commitment and energy. I mentioned how many millions of others there are in the spiritual movement.

Your real work, I told them, will be to find and reach out to those others. To have an impact, you'll have to learn how to cooperate with folks not only from *your* constituency but also from others. Your challenge will be to let go of the illusion that you alone have the truth, that you alone are doing the work, and to open yourselves, really learn from, the hearts, wisdom and energies of others. This work has just begun.

I told them they were *not* the only game in town. I told them that they had hard work to do. But they gave me a standing ovation.

The remarks I had prepared had been what *I* wanted to say. What I said was what *they* needed to hear. I articulated assumptions they probably sensed but couldn't yet articulate. I called them up to a wider perspective. I spoke my truth from the heart. These were of course *my* insights. Yet it was what I felt *needed* to be said. More than I'd ever experienced, the words seemed to flow *through* me, not *from* me. It was as if the vastness was unfurling itself through one heart to another outwards.

I dropped into a pretty settled place during that talk. Speaking real truth seems to do that. And they seemed to drop into that space with me. I spoke very slowly and clearly, which left enough room around each sentence so that we could wait together for whatever wanted to be said next. I meant each of my words; they were surprisingly simple.

I was about as fully *with* those folks in that moment as I'd ever been during a talk. It wasn't terribly emotional, though I often felt close to tears. Nor was it very scholarly, though I had ready access to facts and numbers. It felt more like we entered some co-creative space together and we could have jammed almost anywhere. There was very little resistance from them or me in that room.

It's hard not to connect it with the non-resistance that I'd first felt towards that little highway mile marker or the Yellow Shafted Flicker. It was as if we were all waiting for it to express itself in and through words and sound equipment and 200 wide-eyed faces. I'd swear that the vastness had become our collective consciousness.

I never heard Maharishi, Yogananda, Meister Eckhart or Rumi describe such openness in a group. But I'd bet they knew it well. I know I often felt a sandalwood hush descend over the room when Maharishi spoke. He must have seen it. It was luminous.

Meditation is a personal act. Your close your eyes, you let go inside yourself and you drop into "it". Had I not known some such silence inside, I doubt I could have found it with them. But this was in a group: connecting heart to heart, making love, out loud, in the spaciousness with a room full of strangers.

But let's not kid around. This sort of thing doesn't come automatically with a chest full of inner silence. As in other domains, there is a skill set here too. In my case there were years and years of college teaching and professional talks; they no doubt contributed to allowing the sacred to speak itself. There were also years of psychotherapy—and several depressive weeks on a park bench—beneath its non-needy tone. No, mastery of such a skill doesn't magically appear with a shift in consciousness.

Sometimes illumination does seem to make one a brilliant speaker: think of the brilliance of Maharishi, Deepak Chopra, Ken Wilber, Joko Beck, Ram Dass and Billy Graham. But there's probably a generous dollop of character, wit and luck here. Yet nor can I imagine Deepak or Ram Dass speaking out of the kind of centeredness they exude if they didn't live the spaciousness themselves. Not every enlightened being becomes a great guru. But nor do you become a spiritual master without living the silence: necessary but not sufficient.

Whatever the skill set, I think that the core of what the great spiritual teachers are offering is their degree of openness, their level of consciousness. I think what people were picking up on at Bard was not the words but the quality of the state I'd entered that morning. And I know I couldn't have entered it had they not invited me in somehow. In whatever way we sense these things, they were ready and I answered, and all beyond words.

Consciousness is infectious. For good and for ill, you feel it. That's why Amma, the hugging guru, is so powerful. It's why Eckhart Tolle is so appealing and it's why other teachers can say the same words and not draw the disciples. What music really communicates is the openness of soul. So does art. I swear I can sense with Renoir's consciousness when I stand before one of his landscapes. And it's wider than mine.

This is why wide-open teams, as our Board was in North Carolina, can be so co-creative. Michael's very consciousness opened Phil's from a stuck place; Phil's opened mine and on and on. Each of our openings raises the consciousness of the others, as it were. Like playing good jazz we floated up to a level and a creativity none of us could have found alone. It is like mutual consciousness bootstrapping.

That's what happened that morning at Bard: a mutual freeing, a joint raising of openness, a mutual birthing of the sacred.

The good is freedom, and it wants to flow and flow and flow.[108]

This is one of the lessons of my life. The spiritual task is to make room for it in every domain we live, as appropriate in each sphere. Freedom in our skulls and hearts as individuals. In our friendships and marriages, freedom in our laughter and discovery. In our cubicles, free wheeling co-creativity. And freedom even in the halls of parliament and the squares of our towns.

Freedom, freedom, everywhere.

Part III
Reflecting On It

Chapter 11

Living in It

Standing up Straight in It

I wake up this morning at 7. I am surprised by the chill on my face. The hermitage needs heat. I dress and go downstairs, carrying the notes I scribbled half asleep last night. I put in kindling and blow on the embers. The first flames burst up, sudden and orange. I keep puffing. Flames disappear and rise up, disappear and rise up. I pull up the chair, watch the yellow light lick higher and higher behind sooty glass, and feel the first heat wafting from the open stove door. I fill the kettle and put it on the stove—it'll be hot after I meditate. I pad into the back room, settle down on my violet backjack, and wrap the blanket cozily up to my neck. I look outside to see how much snow fell last night, close my eyes and begin dropping down inside, legs out, legs crossed. My breathing slows…

An hour later I blink open my eyes. I get up creakily; my back is stiff from sitting so long. I pad back over to the stove. The water is boiling now; I spoon in tea leaves. I fish my cup out of the dish drainer, pour in the tea, now steeped, add cream and sugar. The tea washes down my throat, sweet and rich, my morning cup of lifeblood.

Steaming cup in hand, I settle into my writing chair. The pages I brought downstairs from last night are here, so I type them up. I listen for the burbling of barely sensed feelings, and I type them into these words.

Two hours later, my stomach hints. It's time for eggs, more tea, and some fried bread. I cook. I sit in front of the window to eat, and watch gray clouds tumbling over the fields. This leads to boots and coat for a walk down by Patch and Lil Girl's place, who come loping…

There are no transitions here. It's like I never have to stop. I do what is next, and then next, and then next, each step an invitation to the next.

What I feel mostly is non-resistance. There is nothing over-against the walls across the room, nothing between me and the trees outside, nothing resisting the burbles of felt-thoughts. It is as if the answers I seek, these very words in fact, were written long ago, and it has taken me all these years to quiet down enough to hear them.

It is like being pushed from behind.

Anxiety is here too, I see, in the back of my throat, just beneath the surface of my mind. I'm a little worried that that my car might slip down the hill when I go for groceries tomorrow or that I've disappeared off the social grid. Something.

Yes anxiety, my old friend, is here. But mostly what I'm aware of is the uprightness I feel just now. It's as if my feet are planted especially firmly on the floor. I could swear I'm sitting taller.

When silence first dawned behind my neck it was a novelty. I was utterly enchanted with it. I read and I listened and I paid attention and I made sense of it in every way I could. I watched it saturate itself over the years into my head and body and then out through my shoulders and torso and into the world. Eventually I gave up on making easy sense of this strange otherness, and I learned to live out of it as opposed to the other way round. And slowly my life has fallen more and more into its thrall. I suppose that's all we can do when something like this dawns, come to terms with the gift we could not possibly have expected, and learn to live into its rhythm.

In the understated and natural way these things probably always happen, there has been a calling here. It has grown more slowly and more humbly than I would have guessed, as if through a back door. Yet in my own analytical and halting way, I have been learning what it means to serve it. Making tea, walking the dogs, feeling the periodic anxieties, writing these words, somehow all feel like the manifestation of this dropping down and out that has become the fulcrum of my life.

I wouldn't say I'm glad exactly. My life would have been much more straightforward (and probably wealthier) had it been baseball or racing cars or boxes of Styrofoam cups that became my life's work. But this has been mine. And it has the virtue of being, just possibly, real.

I am noticing that old sleepy drooping in my forehead again. It is time to stop. I'll put another log in the stove, pad over to my violet meditation perch and pull the blanket up to my neck cozily. Then I'll close my eyes, legs out, legs crossed, and drop in and down and …

Craving It

I am looking forward to walking up the stone path to my house in a few days. I'm looking forward to a gloriously hard shower and to Yvonne's coming through the door. I feel a little mournful about leaving the smooth elegance I have found here, though I'm ready to finally let out my breath after maintaining the precision it takes to be in a place like this.

What I've discovered here is solitude, not loneliness. They are very different. There's a roundness to solitude, a completeness. Solitude is soft, cozy even. I find it comforting.

Loneliness is sharper, an arrow in the belly. When I first arrived here the loneliness was very sharp. I was afraid and I felt very alone. When my car hung over the icy ditch two weeks later, I felt it again.

Interestingly, both times I felt lonely, I was afraid: of freezing, of failing, of doing damage to my car. I wanted Yvonne — or *someone* — to swoop in and take care of everything.

There's always a longing in loneliness, I suspect. You pine — for someplace soft, for comfort, for someone to save you — for *something*. Loneliness always longs. It longs for tomorrow, for someplace or someone far away. Loneliness lives in the not now, not here.

I was carrying awful bucketfuls of loneliness in my twenties. All the unresolved crud from childhood, all the leftover rage. I was afraid all the time, scared I'd never land a career, scared I'd never have a real friend or find love. In the face of such fear I also longed for someplace not here, someplace far away. I could have longed for fame or love or martyrdom I suppose. But what I longed for was *enlightenment. Mokṣa would be* a different life, faraway, the perfect life with a sharper mind and a healthier body, more loving relationships and, yes, thicker hair. It was my better tomorrow, *the* answer. And I wanted it bad. Enlightenment was *not this, not here.* Enlightenment was "it will be better."

Oh, I'd heard Maharishi talk endlessly about "cosmic

consciousness," the first stage of enlightenment. I had heard tell that when you shift your state of consciousness and live the great silence, you would witness your thoughts and feelings. I studied the video tapes and memorized the phrases until I could recite the descriptions by heart.

But what I heard, really groked in my gut, had little to do with some shift in the relationship between consciousness and its objects. What I heard, and longed for deep in my bones, was that magical shift, that different life, that tomorrow far away. What I longed for was a shift so sweeping that all my troubles would just melt away, and I would be finally, really, happy.

With needs as intense as mine, I suppose, I would have pined with the same intensity no matter what I wanted. Had I continued with the guitar, maybe I would have dreamt of adoring crowds. I would have longed for a governor's mansion had I gone into politics. Had I been a medieval Catholic, perhaps I would have yearned to be the *most* moral, or the *most* helpful, or maybe even a revered martyr. My longings were that intense.

But when that humble silence planted itself in my life, when I got the pot of gold for which I had craved, it wasn't at all what it was cracked up to be. It was not at all instant perfection. No wonder I became so confused and disillusioned! How could I possibly make sense of the terrible fact that, even with the much vaunted silence in my soul as permanently as my own heartbeat, I was still just a hurt and scared little boy?

Had I longed a different longing, the outcome would probably have been the same, give or take. Had I worked hard in the paper business and gotten rich, I probably would have found myself disappointed and confused at 40 about why, "even with all this money," I still wasn't happy. Had I become a physicist or a woodworker, I suspect, it would have been the same story, different tool set.

We come into the world broken. We choose our path and slowly fix our souls, more or less, and we try to become more complete. Musicians, businessmen, wives, ministers, prostitutes, botanists and spiritual teachers are all on a similar journeys, I think, all growing beyond the limitations of their youth, all in their way.

It is the path of the hero I have been pursuing. The way of meditation and reflection has been my path to overcome narrowness and to find rebirth. We all fight our demons, I suppose, whether it be with swords or guns or paint or film. We each seek our grail in our own way. The spiritual and meditative way is just one way, my way, to become whole.

And yet … this seems to miss something. The spiritual life, for all our confusions and our foolish intimations of superiority, the life of ongoing self examination and a commitment to the fully free life may actually be different.

Had I stayed a businessman or become a musician, for example, I would no doubt have been ambitious and worked hard to develop my craft. I would have grown personally a good bit, no doubt. But I would probably never have known quite why I was still so unhappy or what, fundamentally, to do about it. I might have gone to a psychotherapist or found my way to a spiritual workshop run by someone like me, and I would no doubt have made slow, incremental progress. But the inner work of becoming truly free at every level would have always remained an interesting but dubious sideline to my "real" work: the paper or music or teaching business.

Yes, people grow up in every lifestyle. But a serious and lifelong spiritual commitment brings an unexpected overplus, I think. Unlike the paper business or the pilot's life, the whole *point* of the spiritual path is to self-reflect and to let go of everything, anything, to which we cling. "Let go of where you entrap yourself," it whispers. "Good. Now let go even more. … Now do it again."

The spiritual life may be the only life which is *explicitly* about facing and then relinquishing every illusion that has enchained us. Including itself. Unlike the search for money, fashion or power, there is a spiralling of self-transcendences here that has no end.

You answer with your life. You respond more haltingly than you might like, and as best you can. But its calling—to live in ever deeper alignment with truly effortless freedom—never ends. And you cannot not answer.

If it is successful, as mine has been to some extent, it can lead to a life of effortless transcendence, a lightness of spirit we could not otherwise imagine.

But the path we are on is not really about healing anxiety or ending unhappiness. Nor is it about ending rebirth, as many Hindus believe, though it may accomplish that as well for all I know.

No, what silence really brings to a life is a whole other real, a new metaphysical domain in which we come to live. Silence, Brahman, the Tao, Christ Consciousness—these words are pointing to a different *kind* of reality than everything else that we might feel or own or think or hope. Whatever else it might bring, the sacred infuses life with that which is deeply, profoundly *Other*.

Everything we know to hope for is *within* the worldly. Ending depression, owning a Mercedes, gaining bodily health—these are all worldly aspirations. The fame or political power or brilliance or wealth I have sometimes longed for are all within the world. But they are all utterly different in quality and nature than silence itself.

To encounter silence is to encounter a mystery. It is to be handed a secret you did not know you did not know, to find yourself in a story you could not have known how to write. There's buoyancy to life in knowing the secret, a lightness beneath your breath. To know it means that everything you knew, all of this world and this body, stops being the only world there is. You come to carry an unbidden translucence.

And yet, and yet, it is not unconnected with how we be in the world.

Its Fluidity

I watched a small log get caught between two rocks in the half frozen stream behind my hermitage yesterday. It was blocking the flow. The stream billowed and boiled and pushed at it; water ran over and under and around it, streaming and pushing. Leaves and sticks and unrecognizable debris began piling up.

By this morning's walk my little dam had disappeared. The stream no doubt pushed it loose and re-created its own freedom. That's what this spiritual life is all about: free flow; then whenever and wherever it gets blocked, re-creating its flow. And so it goes, until we live freedom, freedom *every*where.

My friend Tom Duffy, a meditator of forty some years, is an outrageously hammy and charismatic leader of the New Hampshire-renowned rock and roll band, "The Effengees: Like a Garage Band only Louder." Effengees' gigs are riots of foot stompin' and humor and power. They're times to dance like no one's watching, to drink a little more than you should, and to belt out "Mustang Sally" and "Go Johnny Go" as loud as you please. I've seen as much joy at Effengees events as I've seen on any meditation weekend. It's probably not as life altering, but gad, those nights are a hoot![109]

During a set break I sat next to a Korean Zen Roshi.[110] I'm quite fascinated by Korean Zen and she seemed lovely sitting there, all primly folded hands, shaved head and silver robe. So I sat down next to her. I asked about her kids. I asked about her Zen center. I asked her with a smile how on earth she kept her robes so crisp?

She responded, quite correct, earnest, slow voiced and monosyllabic. You know: the distant and impenetrable sage act.

It was like chatting with a wall! I never learned where she was born, what she liked, whether she was divorced. And not once did she smile.

After a little while, I gave up. A Zen student soon wandered over and sat on the floor, literally at her feet. Suddenly she was all low register and stately Zen teacher voice. She actually seemed relieved that she could now play Roshi.

Perhaps knowing that a student or two was there cramped her style. And no doubt, I can be a bit much. But honestly, I found her frozen nearly solid, without a shred of personality or vulnerability or doubts or playfulness. There was no way to contact her as a human being, and certainly not as a woman.

I wanted to shake her and shout "Gad, lady! What good is all that sitting if you can't play? This is an Effengees gig, for god's sake! Can't you stop being the Roshi? Come on, let's boogie!"

We spiritual types can take ourselves soooooo seriously, can't we? Christians, Hindus, Buddhists: we can all get so painfully earnest! Can you even picture Maharishi, Muktananda or (oy!) Pope Benedict getting down, loud and happy with the Effengees? (I could see Deepak Chopra maybe, or Ram Dass before his stroke. I'd bet the Dali Lama could do a mean bunny-hop if he'd lose the robes!)

But most of us spiritual types, especially those of us who take on the guru or priestly role, get so into the act, so sober in our sobriety. It's like we're hiding behind our self-appointed "Obi-wan Kenobi" robes.

This is not freedom. It is just another garden variety attachment.

To think that the only "spiritual" tone is serious, deep voiced and kindly is a spiritual blunder of the highest order. If it is anything, the complete life we are or should be after today has to include spreading our arms wide to the whole gallimaufry of human feelings and doings and actings. God save us from some bloodless "joy, joy, joy!" If we are after anything, we are after full-bodied *freedom.* We are after the complete and unhesitant use of head and intellect, stretching from heart and love to head and thought to crotch and animal sex to foot and stompin'. I want to be awake, utterly non-resistant, to pain and joy and love and loss and boredom and knowing and not-knowing, wide open to the full catastrophe that is the paradox of a whole, confusing human life.

What makes a life spiritual is its *range*, for God's sake, not its *sobriety*. Life is movement. The more alive you are, the more flexibility you live. And vice versa.[111] The truly spiritual can flow any-emotional-where without any hesitation whatsoever. Effengees gigs are times for foot stompin', not slow talking; flirting, not sharing dark secrets; and if you're free in all things you can enjoy their outrageous New Hampshire gigs without hesitation. The real spiritual freedom I think we should be after can go deep and serious and funny and raucous and thoughtful and can plan with a spread-sheet, each when the time is right. It can play alne, with another and in a group, even a big one, each without holding back.

Real spiritual freedom lives unhindered, wide open in the juicy paradox that is being a poly-modal human being. We are beckoned by possibility.[112]

It is a deep irony that those who are called "religious" tend to be among the most stuck, the most obsessed. The ultra orthodox Jew, the fundamentalist Christian, the jihadist, the silver robed Korean Zen monk have co-opted the word "religion" and have re-defined it as its very opposite.

The true "religious" are the free, the bendable, the open, the fluid. They alone are the scions of God. People in funny clothes and strange headgear, people who do precisely what their tradition says, people who have stopped being open to the simple humanity of someone on another path or are no longer able to play—these are not the religious, they are the frozen. Such people have taken God and cast Him into their group's very own golden calf. Religion that believes in religion, says Buber, "has become the most exalted form of invulnerability against revelation."[113]

Religion should make us more alive, not less, more flexible, more responsive, not less. That's why Psalm 33 says, "sing unto Him a *new* song," not the same old song sung in the same old way. The soul-jazz-enlightened are the most free, not the most obedient.

Or the most prim. Rather than some distancing "joy, joy, joy" or some pressed-robed "sober, sober, sober," the spiritually free human being is effortlessly open, i.e. *lives jazz in the soul, under any circumstance.*

Lord let me dance to that old rock and roll music *and* sit comfortably on the meditation cushion *and* weep with melancholy and mourning *and* think creatively with my buddies *and* love the gentle curve of a woman's back, each at the right moment.

Don't get me wrong. True human freedom, I'm coming to see, is not some return to a teenage dance-till-you-drop hedonism. Most of us have known how to dance since we were kids and learned to screw long ago, though perhaps not as lovingly as we might. What is new here is the core. Most of us cannot fathom the spacious emptiness to which that prim Korean Zen teacher has dedicated her life. Most of us, frankly, cannot connect with our own depths very well and even less can we connect with the depths of another. Most of us run away from the secrets hidden in silence and hide from the divine spark. The truly spiritual person can access the deepest silence, the most critical intellect, the most painful psychic memory and the sexiest kiss, each equally and each without hesitation.

What I think we should be after, what I'm after, is true freedom, deep and wide.[114] It includes the tears that well up with unabashed love, the easy smile that comes from a fully resolved issue with another, the silence that can only be known by being it, and laughter, real belly laughter at the Rabbi, the Priest and the Minister who walk into a bar. Such Freedom, deep and wide, flows into love when the lights go dim, into mourning when the grim reaper does his deed and gets down, really down, when the Effengees crank up. And in the midst of it all, it is as settled and non-resistant as the wind.

The goal I am envisioning then is, to be effortlessly open, i.e. *to live jazz in the soul, under any circumstance, on the settled ground of spiritual spaciousness.*

Now *that's* a *telos* worth pursuing!

Alone

I took another walk with the dogs this afternoon. It'll probably be my last. The book is nearly done and I'll be leaving tomorrow.

Patch, Lil Girl and I tromped through the knee high snow across the great field and down the long drive to the country lane. Dusk was coming on. The sun was jutting through the clouds, low and polarized. The shadows across the road and up the sides of the weather-beaten barn seemed as if etched with a razor.

I called over to the stoop shouldered farmer, "hey, take a look at your barn!" He looked but just waved, no doubt seeing only aging wood and next year's paint job, and probably thinking I was a coot.

The moment—angular, sharp edged and strikingly clear—was painfully dazzling. But I had no one to share it with except the dogs, who didn't care. My momentary miracle of light and shadow was as lonely as it was magical.

I've often felt that way on the path. The further along I have gone down the road, the fewer the people I've had with whom I could share it. My TM buddies did not share my academic discoveries nor did my philosophical friends share my meditations. Bill Barnard, Scott Lowe, Philip Wexler and a few others shared both, and I used to look forward to conferences where we could have dinner and laugh over our subversively dual lives. But even so, they didn't share my two decades of psychotherapy, nor have I shared their steps into Ayahuasca, alcohol or Yoga. I've never found anyone who shared my sense of non-resistant unity, nor others their shifts with me. No one has done quite what I've done, seen the spirit chiseled into walls just as I have, nor I theirs. There's a poignancy in spiritual progress, an aloneness that goes with the determination that I didn't quite bargain for.

The Forge Institute is a community of the spiritually independent. I have loved dearly Phil, Doug....and others who have been part of it. Holding hands with fellow pilgrims, jamming together as we dance across the great chasm, is one of the privileges of being human. To love and be loved by these people has been a blessing I did not expect. To have my intrepid partner Yvonne and my beloved kids Rosha and Avi walk with me through my strange and self-generated tumblings is another gift I haven't really earned. We have gotten to hold each other's hand awhile, and I am deeply grateful.

But today, watching the shadows sluice across the street like razors, I feel very much alone. Perhaps I didn't share the dawning of silence with anyone back at the Hotel Karina because I *couldn't.* What happens inside your neck or head, or what stretches beyond your shoulders or through the walls, is, in the end, private. It can be described. It can be discussed. But it cannot be shared, not really. In the end there is an aloneness to the human journey, a final, existential solitude.

That's just the deal I suppose. You get to grow and learn and discover who you are, your way. If you keep at it and work through another logjam, you get to take yet one more step. But even if you hold the hand of a fellow pilgrim, you do so alone.

In that deep down place where quarks and electrons are equal, or in that deep level where I yawn in the trees, we are not alone I suppose. It is a comforting thought. But just now, walking down the lane with the dogs snuffling between lengthening shadows, it is the melancholy joy of the path I feel, the achingly beautiful ambiguity that is an increasingly conscious life.

I'd like to add, "yet I wouldn't trade it for the world." But I'm not sure if that's true. Honestly, I wish sometimes that I'd stayed in the Iowa TM community. I'd be less perplexed, for sure, and surrounded still by brothers and sisters who thought and hoped like me. It's a good life, passing your days in a community of empathy with like-minded souls. I miss it terribly sometimes.

But like leaving childhood, finding my way out of the TM world was probably inevitable, of a piece with the existential solitude I'm feeling just now. That simple thought, 'I wonder what I have to say?' was so natural. And so devastating. Growing up in one's own way is not always pleasant. It is definitely not easier. But there is an inexorability to it that makes it seem very right.

It is as if the vastness in my belly and in the sun behind the mountains was beckoning from the start, and has continued to call me to this very place, this very moment. Every time I let go another "must," every time I saw through another picture of the way things "should" be, as I always had to, I took another step both towards the real and towards the freedom that is this deeper solitude of being. Every time I saw another pattern as self-destructive or another choice as out of integrity, I was taking another lonely step into the flow.

In the end we are each alone, I suppose. Alone with the silence, alone with the shadows that chisel themselves across our barns, alone in our struggles and our discoveries.[115] So no, I'm not sure I wouldn't trade my commitment to becoming more aware in exchange for a more upscale job or an enmeshment in a wider community. But I'm also not sure I could.

Rather than happiness, or *ananda*, that stunningly overambitious Hindu word for pleasantness, in the end what you get is to become ever more real. You get to stand bent under the burdens of fewer and fewer of your own lies. With your feet planted ever more deeply into the soil of what is so, you get to become ever more vertical. And you get to discover with and to invite others who wish to do the same.

What the spiritual path offers is not unmingled happiness and it is not the conventional. Nor is it camaraderie or ease, though these may come. What you get instead is to be increasingly open to the joy and the melancholy that is the deeply lived life.

In the end you get to be increasingly alive, the mystery coursing up your spine. You get to be more awake, more deeply honest, freer, and to stand up straighter and straighter in it. You get to be, in all its ancient simplicity, *Homo erectus*.

And today, walking the dogs and watching the shadows softening now across the weather-beaten barn, it seems like an honor to which I've been called here in this snowbound place and through this strange life I have lived.

I have been invited, I think, into the fellowship of the erect.

In return I can do no other than to stand up straight in what I am, and, dear reader, return the invitation to you. I invite you, as I have been invited, into the only *summum bonum* complete enough for today: to stand up ever straighter in every domain of your life in the full mystery that is becoming free, deep and wide. I invite you into the ambiguous privilege that is a life of silence.

Endnotes

1 Bhagavad Gita, A New Translation and Commentary, Chapters 1-6. (NY: Penguin, 1990). p. 165.

2 Gita, p. 174.

3 Gita, p. 371.

4 The Upanishads, trans. Alistair Shearer and Peter Russell, p. 36.

5 The Upanishads, Juan Mascaro, (NY: Penguin, 1985), p. 86.

6 Charles Tart: "Enlightenment and Spiritual Growth: Reflections from the Bottom Up," *Subtle Energies and Energy Medicine*, vol. 14, no. 1, p. 29.

7 ibid, p. 35.

8 This was a phrase that we told each other in those days, and one that Deepak Chopra uses in the Huffington Post, February 13, 2008, 23/6, on the occasion of Maharishi's death.

9 Gita, p. 196.

10 Maharishi Mahesh Yogi on the Bhagavad-Gita: A New Translation and Commentary, Chapters 1-6. (NY: Penguin, 1990).

11 Steven Mitchell, The Enlightened Mind (NY: Harper Perennial, 1991), pp. 51 - 2.

12 Paul McCartney, "Cosmically Conscious," first played on McCartney's solo album, "Off the Ground."

13 The Heart Sutra. Translated from the Korean by Zen Master Seung Sahn. Chanting book, Kwan Um School of Zen.

14 Lama Lodo, *Bardo Teachings: The Way of Death and Rebirth* (San Francisco: KDK Pub, 1982), p. 7.

15 Quoted in Joel Morwood *The Way of Selflessness* (Eugene OR: Center for Sacred Sciences, 2009), p. 29. No attribution

16 William Johnston, The Cloud of Unknowing and Book of Privy Counseling, (NY: Doubleday: 1996), p. 169.

17 Gita, p. 349.

18 Gita, p. 365.

19 Buddhism describes the process of experience and of having a sense of self as made up of *skandas,* generally translated "heaps." All experiences are comprised of these five processes, which constantly churn and change. And our sense of our self as a discrete thing (an I) is so comprised as well. A nice introduction can be found in Robinson and Johnson *The Buddhist Religion,* second edition (Encino CA: Dickenson Publishing, 1977, p. 43 ff.

20. Gita, p. 428.

21 Gita 2.69, trans. Ramanada Prasad

22 To be accurate, we spent half our time in Mallorca and the second half in Fuggi Fonte, Italy.

23 Gita, p. 174.

24 Gita, p. 307.

25 Gita, p. 250.

26 Gita, p. 233.

27 Maharishi Mahesh Yogi, quoted in TM and MUM "benefits" brochure.

28 Gita, p. 371.

29 See the 50th anniversary children's book *Harold and His Purple Crayon* by Crockett Johnson (HarperCollins, 1998.

30 For this insight, and this phrase, I am indebted to John Hunt, publisher extraordinaire.

31 The Enlightened Mind, p. 53.

32 Chandogya 6:9, trans. Alistair Shearer and Peter Russell, p. 75.

33 Nyanatiloka, *Buddhist Dictionary (*Kandy, Sri Lanka, Buddhist Publication Society, 1980), p. 124.

34 Nyanatiloka, *Buddhist Dictionary (*Kandy, Sri Lanka, Buddhist Publication Society, 1980), p. 124.

35 The version Underwood gave us was *The Diamond Sutra and The Sutra of Hui Neng,* trans. A.F.Proce and Wong Mou Lam (Boulder: Shambhala, 1969). There are more recent translations, methinks, but few better. I will put page numbers in the

text.

36 Robert K. C. Forman, Meister Eckhart: *Mystic as Theologian* (Element Books, 1991)

37 He lived, scholars generally hold, from 1260-1328.

38 W 1:41-2

39 James Clark and John Skinner, Meister Eckhart: Sermons and Treatises (NY: Fount Classics, 1994), p. 167.

40 Bernadette Roberts, *The Experience of No-Self* (Boulder: Shambala, 1984),

41 Ibid, p. 20.

42 I should note that, after the onset of this event, she discovered the writings of Meister Eckhart, which she felt did very nearly describe her experiences.

43 Roberts, p. 22.

44 Roberts, p. 34.

45 Roberts, p. 42.

46 Roberts, p 46.

47 See my *Meister Eckhart, pp. 95-125.*

48 See my *The Problem of Pure Consciousness, (NY: OUP, 1990),* and my *Mysticism, Mind Consciousness* (Albany: Suny Press, 1999).

49 Gita, p. 174.

50 Steven Katz, *Mysticism and Philosophical Analysis* (NY: Oxford University Press, 1978).

51. Katz, p. 26.

52. Robert Gimello, "Mysticism in its Contexts," in Katz, ed., *Mysticism and Philosophical Analysis,* p. 85

53. This is a fictionalized account of a meeting with Thomas Nagel, who walked me through a similar set of thoughts. His example was his hobby of spiders, however, about which I know nothing. My apologies to Professor Nagel for ornothizing his arachnology!

54. *Mysticism, Mind, Consciousness* State University of New York Press, 2000. *The Innate Capacity.* Editor. N.Y: Oxford

University Press, 1997. *Meister Eckhart: Mystic as Theologian; An Experiment in Methodology* Rockport Mass: Element Books. 1991. *The Problem of Pure Consciousness* Editor. Oxford University Press. 1990. Articles in numerous journals.

55. If I was doing something that was harming someone or doing something dishonest, I cannot imagine feeling quite so un-conflicted in my work. There would have been some sneaking doubts, however subtle, some pulling back. But in the event I have been lucky enough to work with a kind of settledness of commitment.

56 It was also unusual. I've heard from countless therapists that generalized anxiety disorder has no cure, and that it generally lasts a lifetime.

57 Jack Kornfield, "Sex Lives of the Gurus," *Yoga Journal*. 63 (July-August1985), 26-28 and 66.

58 Jeffry Rubin, *Psychotherapy and Buddhism*: *Towards an Integration,* (NY: Plenum Press, 1996), 88.

59 Raved, Ahiya; Avi Cohen (May 18, 2006). "Rabbi Gafni accused of sexual assault". Ynetnews, retrieved 7/25/08.

60 According to Andishehblog, retrieved October 29, 2008.

61 Karen Terry et al, "T*he Nature and Scope of the Problem of Sexual Abuse of Minors by Priests and Deacons*, prepared by the John Jay College of Criminal Justice (Washington DC: USCCB, 2004).

62 Portions of this paragraph were paraphrased from Chip Brown, "How a Zen Master Found the Light (again) on the Analyst's Couch" *New York Times Magazine* (Ap 26, 2009), p. 37.

63 This is confirmed by a report in the Integral Café blog spot on the work of Jeffry A. Martin. William Harryman reports that in the first study of its kind, Martin is assembling a data base of subjects who report enlightenment. What he finds is that "despite their claims of loss of self, most still take the "I" position in conversation. According to Martin's psychometric

tests, very little about (if anything) about their self is out of the ordinary. They seem to maintain their addictions, their mental disorders, their racial and gender biases, and so on. Those who know them often report no differences in their personalities.

As an aside, he mentioned one person who was taking anti-anxiety medications. This person reported absence of anxiety and appeared to test as such. However, he reported that if he did not take his meds, he would begin shaking and have an anxiety attack.

64 I have seen this tendency even recently in my own and other people's spiritual and religious traditions. I've seen members of many sects deny and try to cover up perceived peccadilloes of their leaders, be those perceptions accurate or not.

65 I am grateful to John Hunt for this phrase and insight.

66 John Welwood "The Psychology of Awakening," Tricycle Magazine, 2000, pp. 43 ff.

67 The exception my be Augustine, who was terribly consciousness of some of his mother issues. But even there I wonder if he got beyond the mom-hagiography.

68 I.e. that the ego is that psychological structure that controls thought and behavior, that remains in greatest touch with external reality, and that is subject to the superego.

69 Steven Katz, "Language, Epistemology and Mysticism," in *Mysticism and Philosophical Analysis,* Ed Steven Katz, (NY: OUP, 1978) p. 39

70 Said first in a private conversation, then during a panel discussion in 1988.

71 As of November of 2009 there were 250,000 Google hits on the Katz Forman Debate.

72 This, by the way, is the theme of the Eminem film "8 Mile." He is able to "win" the rap slam because he welcomes, and even recites aloud, everything that he fears. His dragon, like mine, is left mute, stammering and powerless.

73 Robert Forman, *Grassroots Spirituality: What it is, Why it is*

Here, Where it is going (Exeter,Eng: Imprint Academic., 2004)

74 These more "sublime" perceptions come only when one has held silence for awhile, Maharishi teaches. *The Science of Creative Intelligence: Knowledge and Experience* [Course syllabus], Los Angeles: Maharishi International University Press. pp. 15, 23 -27.

75 Wu-mein, in Steven Mitchell's *The Enlightened Heart*, (NY: Harper, 1989), p. 47

76 Maharishi, Bhagavad Gita, p. 427.

77 Anthony Cambell, *Seven States of Consciousness,* p. 76.

78 Jan van Ruysbroeck, *The Adornment of the Spiritual Marriage,* trans. By C.C. Wynschenk, London, J.M. Dent & Sons, Ltd., 1916. Quoted in W.T. Stace, *Mysticism and Philosophy*, p. 338.

79 W.T. Stace, quoted in Jeffry Kripal, *Crossing Boundaries*, p. 15.

80 Richard Jones, *Mysiticism and Morality*, (Lexington Books, 2004), p. 381.

81 To be quite correct, it was Flavor Aide.

82 I thank DeAnne Cartright for this phrase.

83 *The Cloud of Unknowing*, ed. James Walsh, (NY: Paulist Press, 1981), p. 137.

84 Underhill, Mysticism, p 416.

85 Underhill, Mysticism, p. 417.

86 Walsh, Meister Eckhart, vol. 2, p 105.

87 Maharishi Mahesh Yogi, Bhagavad Gita, p.330- 331.

88 C.J. Jung, Letters, Letter to A. Tjoa and R.H.C. Janssen, quoted by Thomas Moore, *The Education of the Heart* (NY: Harper Perennial, 1997) p. 25.

89 Many Buddhist temples in Asia have rows and rows of Buddhas and Bodhisattvas as objects of worship. But since they are believed to live in different "pure lands" and at different times, they are not interacting as in a group.

90 Kornfield, *After the Ecstasy the Laundry, (*NY; Bantam, 2001), p. xxi.

91 Jack Kornfield suggests Buddha did indeed struggle. He writes, although without a textual reference, about the time Mara, the tempting demon, comes to Buddha, and complains "about how difficult it is to be an evil one all the time. The Buddha listens to Mara's stories sympathetically and then asks, "Do you think it is easy to be a Buddha. Do you know what they do to my teachings, what they do in the name of the Buddha at some of my temples? There are difficulties being in either role, a Buddha or a Mara. No one is exempt." Jack Kornfield, *After the Ecstasy the Laundry,* p. 124

92 See Connie Zweig and Steven Wolf, *Romancing the Shadow: A Guide to Soul Work for a Vital, Authentic Life.*

93 Jack Kornfield, A Path with Heart, p. 6.

94 This story actually was told to me several years before, at an "ISIS" meeting.

95 One Christian record of a group mystical experience comes in *Acts 2,* Pentecost. Quakers sometimes enter into a settled space together, though they share a belief system.

96 Samuel Bonder, Tom Callanan and the Fetzer Institute and Andrew Cohen all speak of enlightened relationships.

97 To be fair, considering the difficulty of writing, some or all may have expressed doubts and just never written them down. Nonetheless, we have no such evidence.

98 *Pace* Pentacost, a purported mutual visionary experience and *Pace* Quakers, who speak of settled meetings, which may be the mutually mystical. But here we have members of a single tradition.

99 Or the single and subjective, the plural and subjective and the single or plural and the objective. Wilber has written about this in many books; a nice introduction is Ken Wilber, *A Theory of Everything* (Boston: Shambhala, 2000), pp. 49 – 53.

100 Muslim female saint of the 8th Century.

101 Olivier and Danielle Follmi, *Offerings* (NY: Stewart, Tabori and Chang, 2003), July 1. Attitbuted to Jack Kornfield, no

reference.

102 An insight I heard in a personal communication from Melissa West, which she attributed to Barbara Fischer.

103 Soshitsu Sen XV, *Tea Life, Tea Mind* (NY: Weatherhill, 1979), p. 77.

104 My friend Suzanne Murphy uses this phrase.

105 Bhagavad Gita, 2:48, 3:19. This is a loose translation, and mine.

106 This is a blues standard written by Jimmy Cox in 1923, and sung by countless folks, but made famous by Clapton in 1992.

107 See p. 162 f. above.

108 The good is freedom, says Soren Kierkegaard in *The Concept of Dread*, trans. Walter Lowrie (Princeton, NJ: Princeton University Press), p. 138.

109 Full disclosure: I joined the band.

110 Full disclosure. I am here combining two separate events. Also, I liked the Effengees so much, I joined the band! And happily belt out Mustang Sally!

111 *Offerings*. 16 August

112 What makes the human distinctive is our range.

113 Martin Buber, *Between Man and Man,* Trans. Ronald Smith (NY: Collier books, 1965), p. 18.

114 Søren Kierkegaard teaches that the goal of human development is freedom: "The good is freedom," he says in *The Concept of Dread*, trans Walter Lowrie (Princeton, NJ, 1944), p. 138.

115 "The threat of isolation [always] accompanies the development of individuality," I read long after writing this in Rollo May, *The Meaning of Anxiety,* (NY: Norton, 1996), p. 375.

Join the conversation about your own experiences,
disillusionments and breakthroughs at
www.EnlightenmentAint.com

Are you in a similar boat as Dr. Forman was?
Have you had experiences you cannot figure out?
Have you been gifted with rich inner experiences but can't seem to find happiness in the rest of your life?
Do you too struggle with the loneliness of the spiritual path?

Dr. Forman is available for consulting, and can help.

Contact him at
office@theforge.org

Why, when my meditative life is so rich, is my marriage so so?
Whey, when I have countless hours on the mindfulness cushion, doesn't my life sing the song of mystery?
With such a Technicolor prayer life, why is my life so grey?
How do I take my spiritual life out of the closet and live it in the rest of my house?

Ever feel this way sometimes? Many of us committed spiritual practitioners do. Hours and years devoted to inner growth and freedom, yet in some ways, we're still troubled, divorcing or downright miserable.

This is the single biggest question for committed spiritual people: I'm so Spiritual, why is my life so messed up?

You'd be amazed how easy it is to fix this, and how much fun.

The Soul Jazz programs.

www.SoulJazzOnline.com

O is a symbol of the world, of oneness and unity. In different cultures it also means the "eye," symbolizing knowledge and insight. We aim to publish books that are accessible, constructive and that challenge accepted opinion, both that of academia and the "moral majority."

Our books are available in all good English language bookstores worldwide. If you don't see the book on the shelves ask the bookstore to order it for you, quoting the ISBN number and title. Alternatively you can order online (all major online retail sites carry our titles) or contact the distributor in the relevant country, listed on the copyright page.

See our website **www.o-books.net** for a full list of over 500 titles, growing by 100 a year.

And tune in to myspiritradio.com for our book review radio show, hosted by June-Elleni Laine, where you can listen to the authors discussing their books.